FIRE FROM
THE SKY

FIRE FROM THE SKY

Essays on the Apocalypse

Lloyd Austin Phillips

WinePress Publishing Mukilteo, WA 98275

"They came up and spread over the breadth of the earth; they encircled the army of the saints defending the Beloved City. But fire came down from the sky and consumed them,"
Revelation 20:9.

DEDICATION

To Jean, my ever faithful companion, who never ceases to give me joy and encouragement in all my endeavors.

I wish to ackowledge with deep gratitude the many persons who, by their prayers and goading, have helped me realize a literary dream which the Lord has given me and enabled me to complete. Special thanks is due Carol Wilfert who, through her patience and great skills, has made visions a reality in the form of a book which I pray will bless many.

CONTENTS

SECTION II: HONOR
Victory For His Beloved City

SECTION III: POWER
Paradise For His Beloved City

EPILOGUE

INTRODUCTION

Opening The Book of *Revelation*

Beginnings are often exciting; but they can also be overwhelming, risky and even confusing. Reading the book of *Revelation* can be all four. It's exciting for those who enjoy the challenge of trying to solve a puzzle that has stumped many. It's overwhelming for those not at all acquainted with the meaning of Biblical symbolism. It is also a risky business for those who expect that somehow the mystery of the great unmarked future will yield its secrets to the assiduous seeker after truth. It's confusing for many who, with good intentions, read it with the aid of respected Bible commentators—saints who in turn understand the book in the light of differing presuppositions which lead them to offer widely divergent interpretations.

Is there a blessing promised to persons reading *Revelation* who may differ in their understanding of the details of the book? God's servant John believed that there was, provided one pays attention to the message that is understood. He wrote, *"Happy is the man who reads this prophecy, and happy are those who hear it read and pay attention to its message,"* Revelation 1:3, Phillips. John concludes the book of *Revelation* with an awesome warning, *"If anyone adds to these words,*

God will add to him the disasters described in this book, God will take away from him his share in the tree of life and in the holy city which are described in this book," Relelation 22:18, 19, Phillips. Let not this warning deter you from reading the book. These words do not promise dire consequences if one innocently cobbles his interpretation of passages in the book; rather, it is a warning to the unbeliever who rejects the message that is understood.

Then, like St. Augustine, hear and heed the words, *"Take up and read."* Preferably read *Revelation* in one sitting; so that its flavor will be felt as you allow its truth to percolate in your mind, and its mysteries to tantalize your spiritual taste buds. Then go back and study its parts in depth, extracting those insights that will aid you, God's thirsty pilgrim, on a journey of faith characterized by a bright and shining hope.

Perhaps as you read *Revelation*, you'll find it refreshing, enlightening, and challenging to read, as I did from *The New Testament in Modern English* by J.B. Phillips. I was so impressed by his Greek scholarship and the beauty of his English, which is not weakened by versification, that I chose in this book to quote from his translation of *Revelation*. Quotes from other books of the Bible are from the N.I.V., unless otherwise indicated.

PRELIMINARY CONSIDERATIONS

Purpose, Date, Destination, Writer, And Themes of *Revelation*

The last book of the Bible is *"a Revelation from Jesus Christ,"* Revelation 1:1a, intended to help readers of the first century see *"what must very soon take place,"* Revelation 1:1b. Because *Revelation* is mediated through Jesus Christ, it also reveals Him; for He is the Victor of the *Apocalypse*. Thus, from this first verse we know that Jesus Christ is both the subject and giver of the revelation. Jesus made known the revelation to John through a mediating angel.

The Greek word translated revelation is apocalypsis which means "unveiling." The book is not intended to conceal truth concerning history's unfolding in Jesus, but to make Him known in His fullness. *"Let every listener hear what the Spirit says to the Churches"* is a recurring admonition given in connection with Jesus Christ's message to the Seven Churches located in Asia, a province in the Roman Empire in the area of modern day Turkey.

In His message to the Seven Churches Jesus not only revealed what would take place in history, He also revealed Himself; for He is the Lord of History—hence the Victor over the forces of darkness and the Church's Salvation!

The first verse also makes clear that the message of the book was first intended for the Christians of the first century near the time of John's exile, in order that they might be prepared to endure when the sufferings alluded to would be intensified. This would seem to place the writing of the book c. 95-96 A.D., during the reign of Domitian.

Revelation makes clear that the extreme persecution known in a limited geographical area during Nero's reign of terror would extend to other parts of the Roman Empire, particularly to the province of Asia.

More severe persecution that would increasingly become psychological, with dire physical ramifications, as illustrated by the banishment of those unwilling to engage in emperor worship, is prophesied. An indication of the demonic and persistent persecution under Domitian is seen in a quotation from I Clement 1:1, in which the writer speaks of *"sudden misfortunes and calamities which have fallen upon us one after another."* These words were written c. 95-96 A.D., during Domitian's rule.

Verse 3 of chapter 1 says, *"The time is near,"* and verse 6 of the last chapter speaks of *"the things that must soon take place."* While these references certainly do not rule out prophecies pertaining to a more distant future, they do indicate that the Lord of the Church was focusing John's attention on what He was doing then in history, which must be viewed in the larger context of God's plan for the consummation of history. That larger context is contained in the last Seven chapters of *Revelation*, although allusions to the larger context are found in previous chapters.

Having said all of the above, it remains true that the words *"Let every listener hear"* highlight truth which makes the contents of *Revelation* not only apt, but essential for all times. Its message of hope, encouragement, comfort and salvation is for the Church of the ages.

The question of the authorship of *Revelation*, though not crucial to the book's message, is more than one of passing academic interest. Many recent Biblical scholars have followed the lead of Dionysius of Alexandria, c. 250 A.D., who ascribed the book of

Revelation to "another John," referred to by some as "John the Presbyter." Those who hold this view buttress their position by citing undeniable differences in style and grammar between the *Gospel of John* and *Revelation*. However, these arguments, I believe, are effectively countered by other scholars. While it is not in the purview of this book to deal with the question of authorship in detail, I do refer the concerned reader to W. Hendriksen's book, *More Than Conquerors*, pp. 15-19.

The clincher for me of arguments for the authorship of *Revelation* by the Apostle John is seen in what James Kallas refers to as a "spiral staircase" approach. Let me illustrate what Kallas means.

John in the Gospel gives us seven signs that point to Jesus as the Son of God. Succeeding signs build on precursors until one reaches the top of the staircase, where the previous steps can be seen from a higher vantage point. A sense of interconnectedness, progress and purpose can thus be seen which gives strength and certainty to truth concerning the divinity of Jesus Christ. Likewise, the visions of the *Apocalypse* each build on that which precedes, going all the way back to seven stars and seven candlesticks or lampstands, the symbolism of which is explained in Revelation 1:20. The truth of Jesus Christ's continuing care for His Church is further revealed through successive images of judgment and conquest, resulting in the establishment of hope grounded in the One who was dead but who now lives forevermore.

This living Christ stands in the midst of the Church giving courage, confidence and hope to those besieged by evil. Indeed, I shall attempt to show that Jesus may be perceived as a "silhouette in His person, life and work" throughout *Revelation*. I am indebted to Jacques Ellul for suggesting that description.

Whereas the grammar and style of the *Gospel of John* support a reasoned approach based on carefully selected materials, *Revelation* in staccato fashion describes fast moving images revealed through visions related to previous images that emphasize truth through visual symbols rooted in the past. These same fast moving images are fashioned by divine insights in the present that must be quickly recorded so as not to lose their impact. This, I believe, accounts for stylistic and linguistic differences between the *Gospel of John* and *Revelation*.

If John the Apostle did not write *Revelation*, then the John who did was so well acquainted with the Apostle's spirit, doctrine and methodology that one must see the *Apocalypse* not quite so much in terms of prophecy related to future events, but more in terms of a pastoral concern that establishes the truth as we know it in Christ with such clarity and power that the Christian community views the cross and all suffering as a means of finally overcoming all evil.

As John, more than the synoptic Gospel writers, saw the way of the cross as a triumphant march to victory; so *Revelation* celebrates the final victory of the Lamb of God over the darkness and destruction of the dragon and its allies, thus preparing the way for the climax of the salvation of His Beloved City, the Church. This anticipated victory makes *Revelation* forever contemporary.

Is there a thematic progression in John's visions which points to the person and activity of Jesus who is revealed in *Revelation* as the Savior of His Beloved City, the Church? Yes, there is. First, in chapter 1 we see Jesus revealed in His "Glory." The revelation of His Glory is pronounced in the first eight chapters. Beginning with chapter nine, which is about Rome's fall, we see Jesus as One worthy of "Honor" through His dominion over evil. This focus of deserved Honor climaxes in chapter 20 with the deliverance of His Beloved City, the Church, and the destruction of the forces of evil. The revelation of Jesus' "Power" exhibited in judgment beginning with verse 11 of chapter 20, and climaxing with the descent of the New Jerusalem and a description of its splendor in chapters 21 and 22, is the final theme of the revelations from and of Jesus.

As a new millennium approaches, it is with renewed interest that we examine the outworkings of God's redemptive purposes in history as set forth in *Revelation*. If this book makes a small contribution to that endeavor, I am grateful.

Let it be known that in this book I focus on the person and activity of Jesus the Lamb, who as Redeemer and Lord takes His

Beloved City, the Church, to be His bride who will *"descend from God out of Heaven"* as the New Jerusalem. In the process of becoming the Savior of His Beloved City, the Church, Jesus brings Glory, Honor, and Power to Himself as the Lamb of God, and thus to the Triune God: Father, Son, and Holy Spirit.

Let Jesus Christ be praised!

"The Polish Rider," Rembrandt van Rijn, c. 1655,
The Frick Collection, New York

What I see in this painting attributed to Rembrandt are the qualities of vulnerability, youthful quest, boldness. I see a sense of mission, albeit the scene begs the question as to whether the mission of the rider will be realized. All of these qualities were present in the young Church of John's day represented by the Seven Churches of Asia to which the *Apocalypse* was directed. Although the art critic Kenneth Clark views *"The Polish Rider"* as a reflection of the horse ridden by Death in Dürer's print of *"The Four Horse-men of the Apocalypse,"* I get the sense from the face of the rider that he will not only endure whatever dangers lie ahead, but will come to the light of fulfillment I see reflected in the sky of the painting. It is this faith that Jesus in His *Revelation* imparts to the Seven Churches of Asia and to the Church of the ages known as His Beloved City.

Jesus At The Center

"They will never again know hunger or thirst. The sun shall never beat upon them, neither shall there be any scorching heat, for the Lamb who is in the center of the throne will be their shepherd and will lead them to springs of living water. And God will wipe away every tear from their eyes,"
Revelation 7:16-17.

Our understanding of *Revelation* will be distorted to the point of forfeiting the blessing promised in Revelation 1:3, *"Happy is the man who reads this prophecy and happy are those who hear it read and pay attention to its message; for the time is near,"* and reiterated by Jesus in Revelation 22:7, *"See, I come quickly! Happy is the man who pays heed to the words of prophecy in this book,"* if we lose sight of the fact that *Revelation* is a revelation from Jesus Christ through His angel and the revelation of Jesus Christ which is described as *"the testimony of Jesus Christ"*. The purpose then of this book is two-fold. First, it aims to help keep our eyes focused on Jesus, the central figure of *Revelation,* that the promised seven blessings of *Revelation* found in 1:3; 14:13; 16:15; 19:9; 20:6; 22:7; and 22:14 may even now be claimed by all whose faith centers in Jesus. The second purpose is to explicate the message of *Revelation* in such a way that the reader may see Jesus, the Lamb, as the One who is the Savior of His Beloved City, the Church, composed of all who have come to know Him as *"King of Kings and Lord of Lords."*

The importance of faith centered in Jesus in John's day was apparent because of the danger that the prevailing Hellenistic culture would completely erode the Christian belief system, making the Church an easy prey of Roman power that sought to solidify its position of dominance by invoking from Christians the offering of allegiance to the Roman emperor—an allegiance of submission and adoration only deserved by God.

Hellenistic culture fostered a philosophy of the unity of all things through the four elements (earth, air, water, fire). The dominate belief was that all things, both animate and inanimate, were permeated by spirit and, as such, could contribute to the wisdom and harmony of life.

In John's day esoteric means of divination were explored in order better to understand and benefit from the complex relationship between the heavens and earth. This approach to experiencing the good life stressed man's efforts in understanding and utilizing the spiritual forces of the universe. According to this view, man using his own devices becomes the master of his destiny.

At its best, Hellenistic philosophy raised life to a higher level of harmony and inculcated an appreciation of ennobling values. However, it failed to understand the profound influence of the demonic which creates chaos and threatens the destruction of even the highest civilization.

Revelation envisions a New Jerusalem wherein righteousness dwells. The New Jerusalem is not a new order created by the wisdom of man; it is a gift from God. John described the gift as follows: *"Then I saw a new Heaven and a new earth, for the first Heaven and the first earth had disappeared, and the sea was no more. I saw the holy city, the New Jerusalem, descending from God out of Heaven, prepared as a bride dressed in beauty for her husband,"* Revelation 21:1-2. The one seated on the throne, according to Revelation 21:5, makes the following pronouncement: *"See, I am making all things new!"* Then in verse seven the voice says, *"The victorious shall inherit these things, and I will be God to him and he will be a son to me."* John's vision of the New Jerusalem not only reveals that the city is an inheritance rather than man's construction; it also identifies the "victorious" as those who are given water "from the fountain of life."

How is it that the people of God receive the inheritance of the New Jerusalem? In John's visions we learn that it is through the mediation of the Lamb that the New Jerusalem descends from God. The Lamb's sacrifice is the means whereby Eden's beauty and harmony are restored. This is seen throughout *Revelation* as the final fulfillment of creation's hope, as stated by Paul in Romans 8:19-21: *"The creation waits in eager expectation for the sons of God to be revealed. For the creation was subjected to frustration, not by its own choice, but by the will of the one who subjected it, in hope that the creation itself will be liberated from its bondage to decay and brought into the glorious freedom of the children of God."* Because Jesus is the hope of all creation, He is worthy of our adoration and worship.

Jesus at the center is the hope of all creation. Jesus the Lamb makes possible the realization of that hope. As you read *Revelation* and this book which tell about the hope engendered by the Lamb, I invite you to behold with me the God-Man of "Glory," "Honor" and "Power" with the aid of the mental image of Salvador Dali's "Christ of St. John of the Cross."

The glory of God and the Lamb, revealed in *Revelation* chapters 1-8, inspires our worship. Note in Dali's painting that Jesus, who was slain before the foundation of the world, is suspended in timeless space. No nails hold His body on the cross. He is held there by the will of God. He is seen in His glory as the central figure of the universe.

The honor accorded God and the Lamb, as emphasized in *Revelation* 9-20:10, is seen in Jesus' position of dominion in the painting. He is without a rival, piercing by the light of His presence the darkness of the abyss that surrounds the cross. The cross is the throne of the Conqueror.

The power of God and the Lamb already holds sway, as seen in Dali's depiction of fishermen protected by the band of clouds from the darkness of the abyss, as they serve the interests of the Kingdom in serene surroundings. Theirs is a precursor position. Soon as, described in 20:11-22:5, the Alpha and the Omega will create paradise, a new Heaven and earth made possible by the victory of the Lamb over darkness, death and the devil.

The cross is the Lamb's vanguard preparing the way for the securing of paradise when the New Jerusalem descends in splendid power from Heaven. Paradise, God's final word envisaged in *Revelation* 21:9-14, will be fully known when the Lamb takes as His bride, the Church. This consummation will be the fulfillment of the Church's hope. Those in whom the Spirit of Jesus dwells have already experienced the descent from Heaven of the New Jerusalem. The New Jerusalem, His Beloved City, will be complete when all of God's elect are in the fold of the redeemed.

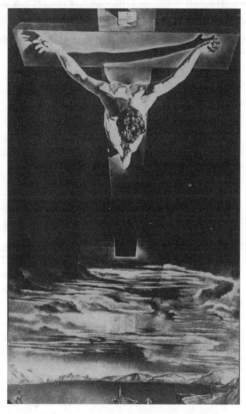

"Christ of St. John of the Cross," Salvador Dali,
1951, Glasgow Art Gallery and Museum

Dali completed this religious masterpiece in 1951. He viewed this crucifixion painting as the result of a spiritual experience. It was inspired by a painting said to have been made by the 16th century Spanish mystic, St. John of the Cross.

"Grace and peace be to you from him who is and who was and who is coming from the seven Spirits before his throne, and from Jesus Christ the faithful witness, firstborn of the dead, and ruler of kings upon earth. To him who loves us and has set us free from our sins through his own blood, who has made us a kingdom of priests to his God and Father, to him be glory and power for timeless ages, Amen!" Revelation 1:4b-6. This word of comfort and assurance was not only given to the Seven Churches of Asia, but also to the Church of the ages, His Beloved City known as the New Jerusalem. The word of comfort and assurance is for all who experience Jesus at the center of their lives.

SECTION I: GLORY
Hope For His Beloved City

Biblical Background for: Jesus, Like A Son Of Man
Revelation 1

Key Verses

"I turned to see whose voice it was that was speaking to me, and when I turned I saw seven golden lampstands, and among these lampstands I saw someone like a Son of Man. He was dressed in a long robe with a golden girdle around his breast; his head and his hair were white as snow-white wool, his eyes blazed like fire, and his feet shone as the finest bronze glows in the furnace. His voice had the sound of a great waterfall, and I saw that in his right hand he held seven stars. A sharp two-edged sword came out of his mouth, and his face was ablaze like the sun at its height,"
Revelation 1:12-16.

1 | Jesus, Like A Son Of Man

In Revelation chapter 1 we learn of the circumstances which gave rise to the visions John received concerning Jesus Christ. His succinct account is as follows: *"I, John, who am your brother and your companion in distress, the kingdom and the faithful endurance to which Jesus calls us, was on the island called Patmos because I had spoken God's message and borne witness to Jesus. On the Lord's day I knew myself inspired by the Spirit, and I heard from behind me a voice loud as a trumpet call,"* Revelation 1:9-10.

Patmos is a volcanic, rocky, mostly treeless island which is ten miles long and six miles wide. It is a Greek island about twenty–eight miles south, southwest of Samos in the Aegean Sea. Banished exiles were sent there by Rome. According to the tradition supported by early Church fathers, John was exiled there (A.D. 95) during the reign of Domitian and returned to Ephesus (A.D. 96). As I write these words, I can hear the breakers splash on the rocky shores of Lake Erie. I can imagine that as John recorded what he saw in his visions, the measured sounds of Aegean waters provided a rhythmic backdrop for his tumbling thoughts as they were quickly recorded.

John's exile to Patmos is not surprising, especially if as an Apostle he exercised a leadership role in connection with the Churches of the province of Asia. He would become a prime target of Emperor Domitian's policies, for he was the first emperor to demand directly that he be worshipped as deity. His high pitched egotism led him to demand that he be hailed as Jupiter's son and heir.

Under Domitian's politico-religious atmosphere, the Christian movement's devotion to an invisible deity opened it to the hostility of an empire ever on guard against inimical entities. In certain localities of the empire Christians were brought to trial and martyred for their faith.

In the light of this unfavorable climate for Christians, the Lord of the Church brought comfort, warning and hope to the Christian Church of Asia, which was already suffering from internal spiritual problems even as it crossed the threshold of grinding psychological testing. John was a great warrior of the faith whose faithfulness to Jesus not only resulted in suffering, but now led to his being chosen by Jesus as the spokesman for His Revelation through the inspiration of the Spirit. The importance and urgency of John's message to the Church of Asia and to the Church of all times can not be overemphasized. An outline of the content of that message, and a sense of its thrust, is already evident in chapter 1 of Revelation.

Domitian's sporadic persecution was a wake up call to the Church. Even those Christians who did not suffer physically felt the pressure of a demonic presence as cultural and economic forces often subtly and persistently threatened to undermine spirituality.

Emperor Nerva, an aged senator, succeeded Domitian, whose rule ended in A.D. 96. Not only did he recall the exiles (John was likely included), but he also released all those who had been imprisoned on suspicion of disloyalty. His brief two year reign brought relief, not only to Christians, but also to other citizens of the Roman Empire. However, Nerva was not capable of keeping warring factions under control. When it became evident that he must choose a successor, he chose Marcus Ulpius Nerva Trajanus, the governor of Germany and his adopted son.

Under Emperor Trajan, his better known cognomen, the empire reached its zenith. Merrill C. Tenney wrote concerning Trajan: *"He was a courageous soldier, a competent administrator, and maintained a strict self-discipline. He adhered to justice in his dealings with his subjects and was free from the capricious excesses of Nero and the rapacity of Domitian. According to the chroniclers of his reign, he was devoid of arrogance and conceit."* [1]

The above quotation would seem to indicate that a respite from persecution was inevitable. Indeed, despite the insecurity of the Church in Trajan's time, it does not appear that it was subjected to constant persecution during his reign. However, the Church's boundaries were well defined. This posed a danger at two extremes which were already present in the Seven Churches of Asia. An indifference and lack of zeal could easily paralyze the Church, as it did in Ephesus, Sardis and Laodicea; or a reaction to even mildly restrictive policies could lead to heretical extremes, which may at least partially account for the heretical movements at Pergamum and Thyatira.

What kind of a revelation is needed for Christians living in an oppressive, restrictive environment where there are pockets of overt persecution and the ever present danger of severe persecution at the hands of a Roman power intent upon using whatever means possible to maintain its dominance? The Church needed the revelation of a Divine Man of Glory who alone is worthy of adoration and worship.

This Divine Man of Glory is described in Revelation 1:13 as *"like a Son of Man"*. Jesus often used this self—designation. "Son of Man" in Revelation 1 is a reflection of the Divine Man of Daniel 7:13 and 10:5-6. The features of John's vision of Jesus would suggest to him, and through Him to the Church, that because this One "like a Son of Man" identified with the Church, no power, not even that of Rome, could compare with the wisdom and power of one whose manhood was endowed with all the attributes of

---

[1] Merrill C. Tenney, *New Testament Times* (Grand Rapids, MI: William B. Eerdmans Publishing Co., 1965), P. 328.

God. Feet of burnished bronze toughened by the fire of suffering were capable of trampling on all the forces of evil. His white hair like wool suggested unsurpassed wisdom and purity. His piercing, discerning eyes would penetrate the sophistry and disguised evil of all the destroyers of the good. And who could forget the authority and dignity symbolized by his long robe and golden girdle? A voice like the sound of a great waterfall resounded with the authority and sharpness of a two-edged sword, declaring both redemption and judgment. This was the Divine Man of Glory *"like a Son of Man" with a "face ablaze like the sun at its height," who held in His right hand seven stars (angels of the Seven Churches of Revelation).* This awesome figure in John's vision stood in the midst of seven golden lampstands (the Seven Churches of the Province of Asia).

Whatever is revealed in all the visions that follow must somehow be seen as a revelation of Jesus whose presence, though at times obscured, is nevertheless a reality. No wonder the powers of evil in John's visions strike out with great fierceness, for the devil knows his time is short. So the voice from Heaven which John heard cried out concerning both the greatness of God's power that resides in the Lord of the Church and the fury of evil: *"Now the salvation of the power and kingdom of our God, and the authority of his Christ, have come! For the accuser of our brethren has been thrown down from his place, where he stood before our God accusing them day and night. Therefore, rejoice, O Heavens, and all you who live in the Heavens! But alas for the earth and the sea, for the devil has come down to you in great fury, knowing that his time is short!"* Revelation 12:10,12.

The Lord of the Church, His Beloved City the New Jerusalem, already in John's day was seen as both a redeemer and judge. After the seventy returned with joy following their proclamation of the nearness of the Kingdom of God, Jesus responded to their report when He said, *"Yes, I was watching and saw Satan fall from heaven like a flash of lightning!"* Luke 10:18.

Through his visions of the Divine Son of Man John emphasizes throughout *Revelation*, but especially in chapters 1-8, that He is the Lord of the Church who reveals God's glory and hence is worthy of worship.

Biblical Background for: Jesus, God's Word
Revelation 2 and 3

Key Verses

"These words are spoken by the one who holds the seven stars safe in his right hand, and who walks among the seven golden lampstands: '. . . To the victorious I will give the right to eat from the tree of life which grows in the paradise of God,'" Revelation 2:1b,7.

2 | Jesus, God's Word

What a treasure for the Church are the messages from Jesus, God's Word, to the Seven Churches of Asia! To the Church of Ephesus He declared that He was holding in His right hand the seven stars, meaning the angels of the Seven Churches. Furthermore, He said that He was walking among the seven lampstands, which according to 1:20 are the Seven Churches. Also, He said to the angel of the Church at Sardis that He was holding the Seven Spirits of God, 3:1.

The messages that came to the Church from Jesus come from One who is fully cognizant of the spiritual leadership and condition of each Church, and One whose Word is empowered by the sevenfold Spirit of God. The words of commendation, rebuke, exhortation and promise carry great authority and hope. The sense of intimacy stemming from the spiritual life imparted to His Church is highlighted by the promises given to the first Church addressed and the last one. He promised those in the Church at Ephesus who repented that they would *eat from the tree of life which grows in the paradise of God,*" Revelation 2:7. He promised the "victorious" ones in the Church of Laodicea that He would eat with them, 3:20. His words are authoritative, for His *"name is the Word of God,"* Revelation 19:13.

Jesus, God's Word, in addressing the Seven Churches in accordance with their special needs and glorious possibilities, indicates what must be done if they are to share the eucharistic blessing of Jesus the Lamb who, John said, *"...loves us and has set us free from our sins through his own blood, who has made us a kingdom of priests to his God and Father, ...",* Revelation 1:5b-6a. The eucharistic blessing is what Jesus has done by the shedding of His blood to make it possible for believers as a *"Kingdom of priests"* to *"serve the living God,"* (Hebrews 9:14). The Church having received this blessing, Jesus' concern now is to show the Church how it can give God the Father *"glory and power for timeless ages,"* Revelation 1:6b. In giving Him glory and power the Church will also be expressing adoration for the Lamb.

Jesus, God's Word, by His exhortations and promises to the Seven Churches of Asia, indicates how they may give the glory and honor due our Triune God now and throughout *"timeless ages":*

Church	Exhortation	Promise
Ephesus	Return to your first love.	You will be given fruit "from the tree of life."
Smyrna	Be faithful to the point of death.	You will be given "the crown of life."
Pergamum	Repent of blind tolerance.	You will be given "hidden manna" (sustenance which the world knows not), and a white stone with a "new name written upon it." (The inscribed stone speaks of divine acceptance and entitlement.)
Thyatira	Renounce apostasy and immorality.	You will be given spiritual dominion, and a new day will dawn.
Sardis	Wake up and reclaim your spiritual heritage.	God and His angels will acknowledge your purity and spiritual revitalization.

Philadelphia	Hold fast to the faith.	You will be given a place of honor as intimate friends of Jesus in the New Jerusalem.
Laodicea	Shake off complacency and strive for the highest and best as disciples of Jesus.	You will be given intimate fellowship with Jesus and the privilege of reigning with Him.

The self-revelation of Jesus in *Revelation* is meant for the edification and encouragement of the Seven Churches of Asia and for Christian Churches throughout the centuries who must deal with problems and evils, much the same as faced the Church of John's day. The following capsule statements call attention to the power and hope found in the Church's head, Jesus, who continues to give Himself for the life of His Beloved City, the Church:

Churches today, like Ephesus, whose fervor and love have cooled, would do well to look at the self-revelation of Jesus, The Alpha, in Revelation 4, as described in this book beginning on page 37.

Churches today, like Smyrna, which suffer from persecution fomented by the devil, would do well to look at the self-revelation of Jesus, The Actor, in Revelation 6, as described in this book beginning on page 53.

Churches today, like Pergamum, which are blinded by the spirit of tolerant eclecticism that undermines the truth as we know it in Christ Jesus, would do well to look at the self-revelation of Jesus, God's Enduring Wisdom, in Revelation 13, as described in this book beginning on page 89.

Churches today, like Thyatira, whose beliefs and practices are threatened by apostasy and immorality, would do well to look at the self-revelation of Jesus, The King, in Revelation 10 and 11, as described in this book beginning on page 75.

Churches today, like Sardis, which are asleep spiritually, would do well to look at the self-revelation of Jesus, the Light And Life, in Revelation 21:22-22:5, as described in this book beginning on page 171.

Churches today, like Philadelphia, which have an open door of opportunity and so need to hold fast to the faith would do well to look at the self-revelation of Jesus, Avenger of God's Holiness, in Revelation 15-16:11, as described in this book beginning on page 107.

Churches today, like Laodicea, which have become complacent because the world is too much with them, would do well to look at the self-revelation of Jesus, Faithful And True, in Revelation 19:11-20:6, as described in this book beginning on page 135.

Revelation is a book of many symbols, but of all the symbols the Lamb is of central importance. The slain Lamb remembered in the celebration of the Eucharist is seen a number of times in *Revelation*; but the victorious Lamb is more prominent. Those who forget this are apt to interpret *Revelation* primarily as a book of prophecy or history, or a combination of the two. While both prophecy and history are present in *Revelation*, they must always be seen in relation to the victorious Lamb who makes possible the restoration of Eden for the sake of Jesus' Beloved City, the Church, which is seen in its perfected beauty in the New Jerusalem.

It is through the adoration of the Lamb that the Church gives glory and honor to the triune God. The Lamb, in giving honor to God by conquering the powers of evil and redeeming the Church, has earned the adoration of all of creation which will fully be given when Jesus returns in power and great glory with His holy angels, II Thessalonians 1:6-10. When this occurs, the promises of Philippians 2:9-11 and Romans 8:19-23 will be realized.

Thus *Revelation* is seen as the drama of God's eternal plan of salvation. This drama is portrayed with great power and beautiful splendor by the great Van Eyck painting, "The Adoration of the Lamb," which is part of The Ghent Altarpiece in the Cathedral of St. Bavon, Ghent, Belgium.

The painting depicts the dawn of a new day. The eye is drawn to the white Lamb standing on an altar. Blood from the breast of the Lamb flows into a chalice, and angels holding the cross and the column at which Jesus was scourged surround the altar. Over the altar and Lamb the dove of the Holy Spirit sheds golden rays. Left of the altar a group of confessors advances from the groves, and on the right of the altar martyrs bear palms. In the center forefront, below the altar, the Fountain of Life pours water from golden spigots into an octagonal basin. This reminds one of *"the river of the water of life, sparkling like crystal as it flowed from the throne of God and of the Lamb,"* Revelation 22:1. To the left of the Fountain of Life are kneeling prophets holding their books, while behind them are standing patriarchs and kings from the Old Testament. On the right of the Fountain of Life are kneeling apostles in front of standing saints. Not to be missed in this painting, depicting the relationship between the various groups to the victorious sacrificial Lamb who has provided His blood for the Eucharist and the Water of Life for our salvation, is the natural setting and background skyline. The emerald-green meadow of Paradise, with its wild spring flowers and the presence of Easter daisies, orange trees and roses, is Eden restored by the Lamb. In the background is a ridge of dark hills. Behind them is seen the New Jerusalem against a skyline of bluish mountains. This city, holy Jerusalem, is the bride, the wife of the Lamb, (Revelation 21:9-10).

Finally, note that in the Lamb's Beloved City, whose spires are seen in the distance of Van Eyck's painting, *"The Adoration of the Lamb,"* there is no external light for: *"The city has no need of the light of sun or moon, for the splendor of God fills it with light, and its radiance is the Lamb,"* Revelation 21:23.

Van Eyck's Lamb, like John's depiction of the Lamb in his visions, is seen as central to the understanding of *Revelation*. His view of the Beloved City, like John's, depicts the restored beauty of Eden.

"Adoration of the Lamb", Jan and Hubert Van Eyck, 1432,
St. Bavon, Ghent

Biblical Background for: Jesus, The Alpha
Revelation 4

Key Verses

"And whenever the living creatures give glory and honor and thanksgiving to the one who sits upon the throne, who lives for timeless ages, the twenty-four Elders prostrate themselves before him who is seated upon the throne and worship the one who lives for timeless ages. They cast their crowns before the throne and say, 'Thou art worthy, O Lord our God, to receive glory and honor and power, for thou didst create all things; by thy will they existed and were created,'" Revelation 4:9-11.

3 | Jesus, The Alpha

The divine thrust towards harmony and beauty so present in the imagery of Revelation 4 is evident throughout the book of *Revelation*. The seven lamps blazing, which are seven Spirits of God, (Revelation 4:5), perfection at its highest, gave a dynamic presence to the beauty of the rainbow, resembling the brightness of an emerald which encircled the throne.

What a fitting setting John saw for the One sitting on the throne who had the appearance of jasper and carnelian. Twenty-four thrones with twenty-four Elders seated on them surrounded God's throne. They were dressed in white and had on their heads crowns of gold. What appeared to be a sea of glass as clear as crystal was before the throne.

This grandiose vision of the spirit world which John saw through the door opening into heaven would never leave him, even in those times when out of the darkness of the abyss hideous foes would emerge threatening to destroy the Church, His Beloved City, which is the New Jerusalem in its incipient form.

This first vision of harmony and beauty opened up for John the world of Jesus the Alpha, *"the very first to rise of all who sleep the sleep of death,"* I Corinthians 15:20. The living creatures exhibiting the highest roles of creation as represented by the king of the jungle, the lion; the greatest beast of labor, the ox; the one given dominion over the earth, man; and the flying eagle, which soars the highest, all join in the chorus of praise to the triune God, saying, *"Holy, holy, holy is the Lord God, the Almighty, who was, and is, and is coming,"* Revelation 4:8.

Jesus the Alpha is also Jesus the Omega, God's finality, in 1:8,17; 2:8; 21:6; 22:13. Like God who sits on the throne, He too is worthy of the worship of every creature in all of God's creation, 5:11-14. The ascription of praise was given to the Alpha and Omega, the First and the Last of the Church, even Jesus whose blood *"purchased for God, men from every tribe, and tongue, and people, and nation!"* Revelation 5:9. With the One sitting on the throne, He, *"the Lamb who is in the center of the throne,"* Revelation 7:17, is worthy to receive glory and honor and power.

The throne room scene in John's vision was a scene that Jesus, the Alpha who gave birth to the Church, wanted John to impress on the minds of the persecuted Christians in the Seven Churches of Asia. In visions of the workings of evil that would follow, the Alpha who is coming was ever to be seen in human history as the one in control of the destinies of the human race. He will ever be the head of His Church, even as He is the one worshipped by heaven's creatures. *"Keep this scene of splendiferous beauty ever before you,"* He was saying to the Church of all ages, *"so that when the hard days come, there will always be the confidence that harmony, order, and beauty will one day be supreme everywhere."* How do we know? We know because the throne mentioned seventeen times in chapters 4 and 5 is His throne of dominion. We know because the key creatures of creation who became symbols for four sons of Jacob were the ones offering God and the Lamb the highest ascription of praise night and day.

Judah, who had lion-like eminence and might suiting him for leadership of great magnitude, offered praise. Reuben, the man of tender compassion who gave Leah mandrakes, popularly known as love apples, offered praise. Ephraim, who was the ancestor of spiritual giants such as Joshua, Deborah and Samuel, and who with the strength of the ox often bore the brunt of preserving God's people, Israel, offered praise. Dan, who like an eagle, flew untouched high above the Amorites and Philistines, offered praise. The Seven Churches and the Church of the ages should take comfort in knowing that the spiritual qualities of God which He imparts to His people assure them of survival, despite the oppression of evil. The Alpha, God's only begotten Son, has begun a good work in His people and will complete it, Philippians 1:6, because with the Father and the Holy Spirit He occupies the throne high above all the principalities and powers of evil.

The ascription of power and holiness to the Alpha, who from the throne superintends the creation and protects the Church He has formed, was accentuated and thus fixed in memory by peals of thunder and flashes of lightning, 4:5. Over the throne was the rainbow, ever a symbol of hope. The glass–like sea which John saw was a symbol of peace, assuring the believer of the forgiveness and cleansing in the laver of the grace of *"Him who loves us and has set us free from our sins through his own blood,"* Revelation 1:5b.

This throne room scene of John's vision is not one that is to be contemplated and enjoyed like a masterpiece painting. Rather, it is one in which troubled and persecuted Christians can participate when they are going through deep waters, much like the Navajo Indian participates when a sand painting is being created. The sand painting is not created to last; but it becomes an environment of beauty and harmony in which the creator lives and acts constantly. The Church through its worship, and individual Christians through throne room imagery, are given the spiritual reinforcement that the vision of John in Revelation 4 supplies. We who have tasted the fruit of God's grace need to experience vicariously the revelation which John described in the words, *"Later I looked again, and before my eyes a door stood open in Heaven, and in my ears was the voice with the ring of a trumpet, which I had heard at first, speaking to me and saying, 'Come up here, and I will show you what must happen in the future,'"* Revelation 4:1.

Let the "voice with the ring of the trumpet" be heard as we experience beauty, harmony and beatitude by beholding the Man of Glory, Honor and Power, who imparts hope to His Church. Jesus the Alpha, who secured our salvation through the shedding of His blood, is worthy of our deepest devotion, our heart-felt adoration, and our sincere worship. We are members of His Beloved City, *"the Church of the firstborn, whose names are written in heaven,"* Hebrews 12:23a.

But where is Jesus mentioned in Revelation 4? If there is no direct mention of Him in chapter 4, on what basis would anyone discern Him in that context to be the Alpha who is first and foremost in the life of the Church? The answer is profoundly stated in Jesus' words to the Church at Laodicea: *"As for the victorious, I will give him the honor of sitting beside me on my throne, just as I myself have won the victory and have taken my seat beside my Father on his throne,"* Revelation 3:21. Where God the Father is on His throne in Paradise, there Jesus is also. He is there as the Alpha who has triumphed over evil. Therefore, to His victorious followers He will give the honor "of sitting beside" Him on that same throne. As I have also indicated, *Revelation* is a revelation from and of Jesus. Therefore, we would expect, as Ellul's metaphor "silhouette" suggests, to perceive His presence throughout *Revelation*. His presence is silhouetted in chapter 4 by the Twenty–four Elders who, in response to the four living creatures (a high order of angelic beings), "....give glory and honor and thanksgiving to the one who sits upon the throne..", 4:9, *"..prostrate themselves before him who is seated upon the throne and worship the one who lives for timeless ages. They cast their crowns before the throne and say, 'Thou art worthy, O Lord our God, to receive glory and honor and power, for thou didst create all things; by thy will they existed and were created,'"* Revelation 4:10-11.

Elders throughout the scriptures refer to men given administrative and pastoral roles in the Church. The Twenty–four Elders represent the Church, possibly the twelve patriarchs of the Old Testament and the twelve apostles of the New Testament. As men representing the Church they respond in John's vision to the acts of worship by angelic beings, who, as I mentioned, display worthy characteristics of four of the patriarchs, characteristics of eminence, compassion, might, and spiritual grandeur, which were honored by the Twenty–four Elders as they engaged in acts of worship. These Elders were not only priests offering praise, but also kings who cast their crowns before the throne. With Jesus Christ they belonged to a Melchizedek priesthood—hence the crowns and the thrones on which they sit. Melchizedek is described in Hebrews 7:1 as, *"king of Salem and priest of God Most High"*.

From the above paragraph we see in what sense Jesus is Alpha in His life and ministry within the Church. Alpha is the first letter of the Greek alphabet. Jesus is the first priest after the order of Melchizedek. He is like the mysterious person Abraham met who was in reality a Christophany (Old Testament appearance of Jesus the Messiah). As such Jesus, the Alpha, is *"king of righteousness"* and *"king of peace,"* Hebrews 7:2. He is the *"Son of God"* and a *"priest forever,"* and is *"without father or mother, without genealogy, without beginning of days or end of life,"* Hebrews 7:3.

The Twenty–four Elders representing the Church of John's day and the Church of the ages are kings and priests in the line of Jesus the Alpha, the first priest in the order of Melchizedek. Now this amazing truth comes to light. All the followers of Jesus are spiritual kings and priests. God has given them dominion over the forces of darkness, and they are God's representatives on earth. What a responsibility, but what a lofty calling!

Nowhere is the God-given status of His children more evident than where they join with the hosts of heaven, including the Twenty–four Elders, in worshipping God and the Lamb. Wherever the Twenty–four Elders of the Church Triumphant in Heaven and the believers of the Church Militant on earth worship, there Jesus, the Alpha, is present, even as He said: *"For where two or three come together in my name, there am I with them,"* Matthew 18:20.

With Jesus, the Alpha who gave birth to the order of Melchizedek in our midst, let our worship be responsorial as was the worship of the 24 Elders who responded to the worship of the four living creatures. As kings and priests, together with the Twenty–four Elders, we shall behold the spiritual qualities of God reflected in Judah the Lion, Reuben the Man, Ephraim the Bull and Dan the Eagle, when we offer our sacrifices of praise and lay our crowns before His throne. When confronted by the demonic powers of evil, it is this corporate worship attuned to and responding in like manner to the heavenly beings that will give to the Church the courage, power and perseverance essential for survival and victory. This is why I regard chapter 4 to be the seminal chapter of *Revelation*. It suggests a general outline of *Revelation* in the words *"glory, honor and power,"* as noted in my introduction; but more importantly, it points to the Church's powerful resource of worship, as set forth by the heavenly worship paradigm. It is through its heart-felt, God-centered worship that the Church of our day can retain its first love, the love which the Church of Ephesus had lost.

Biblical Background for: Jesus, The Church's Advocate
Revelation 5

Key Verses

"Then I noticed in the right hand of the one seated upon the throne a book filled with writing both inside and on its back, and it was sealed with seven seals. And I saw a mighty angel who called out in a loud voice, 'Who is fit to open the book and break its seals?' And no one in Heaven or upon earth or under the earth was able to open the book, or even to look at it. I began to weep bitterly because no one could be found fit to open the book, or even to look at it, when one of the Elders said to me: 'Do not weep. See the lion from the tribe of Judah, the root of David, has won the victory and is able to open the book and break its seven seals,'" Revelation 5:1-5.

4 | Jesus, The Church's Advocate

John, the observer and reporter, now became more emotionally involved in the revelation of Jesus given to the Church. As reported in chapter 5, when John beheld the book which contained God's plan for His people, the Church, his pastoral heart became apparent as he "wept bitterly" due to the fact that no one could open the book which was sealed with seven seals. Weeping was his response to a mighty angel who called out in a loud voice, *"Who is fit to open the book and break its seals?"* John observed, *"And no one in Heaven or upon earth or under the earth was able to open the book, or even to look at it,"* Revelation 5:2-3. Then came the response of an Elder to John's weeping, *"Do not weep. See, the lion from the tribe of Judah, the root of David, has won the victory and is able to open the book and break its seven seals,"* Revelation 5:5.

Jesus was worthy to open the book because He earned the right to be the Church's Advocate through His victory on the cross over all the forces of evil. The opening of the book not only made possible an understanding of the Church's future, but it also assured John, and through him the Church, that Jesus would continue the battle with evil until the victory of the cross was realized in its totality throughout the universe.

The final victory for the Church was visualized in the description of Jesus, the Advocate in which John saw a Lamb *"standing in the very center of the throne."* The Lamb *"seemed to have been slaughtered, He had seven horns and seven eyes, which are the seven Spirits of God and are sent out into every corner of the earth,"* Revelation 5:6. That the battle would be the Lord's was seen in that an un-war-like creature, a Lamb (not a lion), with the marks of the cross still evident, was, nevertheless, perfectly equipped (seven horns) to do battle with the Church's fiercest foes. Also, the Holy Spirit in His fullness (Seven Spirits of God) was present with His all discerning laser-like eyes. Jesus, the Church's Advocate was seen as One who would do battle for His own in *"every corner of the earth"*.

But how can we really be sure that Jesus will be victorious? We may be certain of this because Jesus is the magnetic reality of the universe. Jesus dwells in the realm of eternity from which He maintains the phenomenal world which we are accustomed to think of as firm and real in an independent sense, which in reality it is not. The maintenance of our material world by Jesus, the timeless One, is stated in the words, *"He is before all things and in him all things hold together,"* Colossians 1:17. When one accepts this mystery, it is not surprising to learn that some physicists like David Bohm argue that there is an overarching order responsible for the order we perceive as either being present or missing.

This overarching order is evident in *Revelation*, even in those horrendous situations where evil appears dominate. From a position of complete supremacy, Jesus the Advocate of the Church does not allow anything to occur in our earthbound lives which can not somehow serve a spiritual purpose in keeping with God's will. This truth, as it applies to God's people, is stated with engaging certitude in Phillips' translation of Romans 8:28: *"Moreover we know that to those who love God, who are called according to his plan, everything that happens fits into a pattern for good."* John's banishment to Patmos was a good illustration of this truth. His role as a seer of visions prepared him to be an interpreter and proclaimer of truth seen to the Church.

Every Christian is tested and needs the assurance of Romans 8:28. In times of severe testing, God often uses an interpreter to affirm God's Word. This occurred for me when I was seventeen–years old. I was near having my physical life snuffed out. In a fever-induced delirium I saw what I imagined to be an evil eye looking at me as it moved in concentric circles. My mother told me that this was none other than the eye of God watching over me. Recovery resulted. John assured the Church through the *Revelation* of Jesus the Advocate that He is at work on behalf of the Church in the most frightening of circumstances, bringing about the issue of the good. This deeper level of reality beneath the seen centers in Jesus connecting us with another world from which our world is given meaning.

In the world that John discovered through visions the ordinary laws of time, space and motion did not apply. Time and space were in flux as the past, present and future folded into one another. Everything that John saw in his visions pertaining to the conflict between good and evil on earth he keenly felt in the depths of his own being. John experienced not only the reality of that conflict, but also the final revelation of Jesus Christ. He entered into the spirit realm in which the fullness of Jesus Christ was known. From that perspective it was possible for him to affirm what Einstein believed when he said, *"God does not play dice with the universe."*

Everything that John saw in his visions of the seven seals was, or would be, experienced by the Church within the context of the earth's tribulation. The Gospels are very clear in their emphasis of the truth that even the dark side of the Church's life, especially the suffering associated with our Lord's passion during Holy Week, was a fulfillment of God's plan of salvation for His Church. So also the judgments associated with the opening of the seven seals would somehow serve God's redemptive purposes.

Note that the Lamb was the One accounted worthy to break the seals, which in John's vision ultimately resulted in the victory of the countless host of the redeemed, even in the face of the relentless scourge of the evil poured out on the earth. The dominant symbolism of the revelation of Jesus in the book of *Revelation* is that of the Lamb.

In the Old Testament lambs are associated with atonement, which makes possible the forgiveness and victory of God's people. Thus, the Lamb, who is mentioned twenty-nine times in *Revelation*, is worshipped and adored by all things created, as we read in Revelation 5. The worthy atoning Lamb, who is the Advocate of the Church, is ever mindful of the suffering of the Church, and indeed uses that suffering as a means of causing His purified people to fulfill God's saving purposes. Along with Jesus' Shepherd image in Revelation 7, His Lamb image is God's encouragement to the Church, which in John's day found itself facing the possibility of a bleak future due to the rising tide of animosity directed against the followers of Jesus by Roman authorities and demonic powers.

Deep, sincere and Spirit–directed worship was especially vital to the survival of the Church of John's day, because in such troubled times it needed the unity which only comes when the Body of Christ is closely united by bonds of love and devotion to its head, Jesus. Worship was a prominent part of John's visions in *Revelation*. The Divine Son of Man, Jesus, was the supreme object of that worship. God's glory was then, and is now, manifested through the worship of the Lamb in heaven and on earth.

The seven Spirits of God mentioned in *Revelation* 1, 4 and 5 are the Holy Spirit in His sevenfold fullness. The sevenfold Spirit of God is imaged by the seven lamps of fire burning before His throne which are mentioned in 4:5. The four living creatures suggest that everywhere—north, south, east and west—the ubiquitous presence of His Spirit is known and experienced.

It has been noted by some commentators that the Twenty–four Elders not only represent the Church, but that their number also corresponds to the divisions of priests mentioned in I Chronicles 24, and the twenty–four divisions of singers in the Temple referred to in I Chronicles 25. Thus, Twenty–four Elders who *"prostrated themselves before the Lamb"* would likely remind John's readers of the worship order under the Old Covenant.

As the heavenly host worshipped, John noted that not only did each living creature and Elder have a harp, but also each had a golden bowl full of incense, which represented the prayers of the saints. Are not these prayers the key to the triumph of the Church over the forces of evil? Hence the Lamb, who answers prayer and intercedes on behalf of the Church as its Advocate, received the ascription of praise in John's vision when John heard the voices which he described as *"myriads of myriads and thousands of thousands, crying in a great voice, 'Worthy is the Lamb who was slain, to receive power and riches and wisdom and strength and honor and glory and blessing!'"* Revelation 5:11-12. This *"new song"* continues to reverberate in the Church's worship today.

Praise be to Jesus, the Church's Advocate! The slain Lamb by His blood *"purchased for God men from every tribe, and tongue, and people, and nation!"* Revelation 5:9. Therefore, God's people, His Church, have become a *"kingdom of priests for our God, and they shall reign as kings upon the earth,"* Revelation 5:10. Everything that follows in *Revelation* is an account of the victory of the Church over Satan and all his evil allies, making possible the reign of God's people.

Revelation 5 concludes with a glorious paean to the Church's Advocate, the Lamb, which echoes the truth of Philippians 2:10-11. The words of universal praise are: *"Blessing and honor and glory and power be given to him who sits upon the throne, and to the Lamb, for timeless ages!"* Revelation 5:13. *"The four living creatures said, 'Amen', while the Elders fell down and worshipped,"* Revelation 5:14.

Biblical Background for: Jesus, The Actor
Revelation 6

Key Verses

"Then I watched while the Lamb broke one of the seven seals, and I heard one of the four living creatures say in a voice of thunder, 'Come out!' I looked, and before my eyes was a white horse. Its rider carried a bow, and he was given a crown. He rode out conquering and bent on conquest,"
Revelation 6:1-2.

5 | Jesus, The Actor

The opening of the seven seals by the Lamb in Revelation 6-8 is a story of the means the Lamb uses to awaken persons, particularly the Church, to the need of repentance and obedience. The opening of the first seal, resulting in the coming forth of the white horse, points to the fact that the Lamb has a redemptive purpose in mind.

The fait accompli of the Lamb's action is seen in that the figure who came forth when the first seal was broken and a living creature thundered, *"Come out!"*, was Jesus Himself riding on a white horse and holding a bow. He was given a crown of victory and went forth to conquer.

This vision of John portrays the actions of the triumphant Jesus and is an anticipation of what is described in 19:11-16. What follows as the other six seals are broken by the Lamb is a vision of an evil world that brings judgment on itself, a chaotic world in which the Church is tried and sanctified.

Jesus, The Actor in John's vision, creates and controls the context in which this occurs as the Lamb breaks succeeding seals.

55

This is in keeping with the spirit of His advocacy prayer for His disciples and for the Church that would believe in Him "through their message." He prayed, *"My prayer is not that you take them out of the world but that you protect them from the evil one. They are not of the world, even as I am not of it. Sanctify them by the truth; your word is truth. As you sent me into the world, I have sent them into the world. For them I sanctify myself, that they too may be sanctified,"* John 17:15-19.

As John's vision continued, the second seal was broken by the Lamb and a second living creature cried, *"Come out!"* A rider came forth on the red horse of war. He was given power *"to deprive the earth of peace,"* and *"a huge sword was put into his hand."* Out of disruption and chaos caused by wars and rumors of wars throughout history persons have been drawn to a closer walk with the Lord, as they have realized with General Douglas MacArthur, *"It must be of the spirit if we are to save the flesh."*

Another rider on a black horse responded to the Lamb's opening of the third seal when a third living creature said, *"Come out!"* The scales in the rider's hand were a reminder that during a famine persons are forced to portion their food carefully. Exorbitant food prices are seen as indicative of the serious shortage of food staples. Even so, oil and wine are seen in good supply.

Is this not a symbolic reminder that God's ability at such times to supply His own with even less needed items that bring gladness is not lacking? This is Cana-like grace that goes beyond mere survival. The mitigating hand of Jesus at work sparing His own is also seen in Revelation 7:2-3, *"Then I saw another angel ascending out of the east, holding the seal of the living God. He cried out in a loud voice to the four angels who had the power to harm the earth and the sea: 'Do no harm to the earth, nor to the sea, nor to the trees until we have sealed the servants of our God upon their foreheads.'"*

The fourth horse that emerged in John's vision was sickly green in color. John recorded in verse 8 of chapter 6: *"The name of its rider was death, and the grave followed close behind him. A quarter of the earth was put into their power, to kill with the sword, by famine, by violence, and through the wild beasts of earth."* Though the devastation caused by the rider of death in John's vision was awful, the fourth seal was not the last one the Lamb would open. The *Revelation* of Jesus

Christ recorded by John was given to warn, but primarily to offer hope and encouragement.

What hope and encouragement is there in the face of death and the grave? Remember the words of Jesus in Luke 21:28: *"When these things begin to take place, stand up and lift up your heads, because your redemption is drawing near."* The opening of the fourth seal is reminiscent of Ezekiel 14:21, which reads, *"How much worse it will be when I send against Jerusalem my four dreadful judgments—sword and famine and wild beasts and plague—to kill its men and their animals!"* But remember, the opening of the first seal made known God's promise. John saw Jesus as *"He rode out conquering and bent on conquest."* Thus, the promise of victory is given to the Church even in the face of death.

The realization of the promise of victory over death was made possible by our Lord's crucifixion, as the writer of Hebrews declared: *"Since the children have flesh and blood, he too shared in their humanity so that by his death he might destroy him who holds the power of death, that is, the devil—and free those who all their lives were held in slavery by their fear of death,"* Hebrews 2:14-15. The fulfillment of the promise is already seen taking place even as the angel took the censer and mingled its incense with the prayers of the saints and hurled it upon the earth, causing *"thunderings and noises, flashes of lightning and an earthquake,"* Revelation 8:5.

The promise of the first seal was affirmed when in John's vision he saw the fifth seal opened by the Lamb. At this point it becomes clear that the Lamb by opening the seals is making known how God's redemptive plan and purpose is to be revealed through Jesus, The Actor.

Following His death on the cross, Jesus through the Spirit descended into the realm of Spirits captive to death, where He proclaimed victory over death through His resurrection which brought all powers under His authority, I Peter 3:18-22. That assurance of victory over death was affirmed in John's vision, when each martyr received a white robe symbolic of their victory as overcomers, even as had been promised to a few people of Sardis, 3:4-5.

The fact that the first horse had as its rider Jesus, who was depicted as a warrior king wearing a crown and carrying a bow, is a reminder that He is in control of the destinies of His followers on earth. What was true for the Church triumphant in Heaven would also be true for the Church militant on earth. Jesus heard the cry of martyrs in Heaven for justice and told them *"to be patient a little longer, until the number of their fellow servants and of their brethren, who were to die as they had died, should be complete,"* Revelation 6:11.

The opening of the sixth seal by the Lamb is reminiscent of what Jesus had to say concerning the end times, as recorded in Matthew 24, Mark 13, and Luke 21. Though the events prophesied are described as expressions of the wrath of the Lamb, Luke speaks of Jesus' *"Even so"* in Luke 21:31: *"Even so, when you see these things happening, you know that the kingdom of God is near."*

The falling of the stars, indicative of the inability of Israel's religious establishment to forestall the destruction of Jerusalem by Rome in 70 A.D., and the obscuring of the light of sun and moon, indicative of the failure of Israel's leaders to apprehend what would bring them peace, Luke 19:42, had already taken place at the time of John's vision.

The ensuing fear and disruption of orderly life under the leadership of authoritative figures as seen in John's vision, is a reflection of Hosea's prophecy in Hosea 10:1-8. Indeed, lesser gods, those vaunted principalities and powers to which man often has given his allegiance in the hope of securing a felicitous destiny, are unable to aid their devotees of every station in life who cower under the wrath of the Lamb and flee for cover.

From the throne of Revelation 4 judgment must come before liberty and hope can be a reality in the life of God's creation. So that freedom and hope may be realized, the Lamb only gives to death and the grave in John's vision power over a quarter of the earth to kill by the sword, famine, violence and wild beasts.

The message of Revelation 6 is that Jesus, The Actor, is at work even in the midst of earth's tribulations. To the Church her Lord says, *"Let every listener hear what the Spirit says."* And to all the faithful Jesus, The Actor, says what he said to the Church in Smyrna: *"Be faithful in the face of death and I will give you the crown of life,"* Revelation 2:10c.

Biblical Background for: Jesus, Israel's Salvation
Revelation 7 and 8

Key Verses

"I heard the number of those who were thus sealed and it was 144,000 from every tribe of the sons of Israel... When this was done I looked again, and before my eyes appeared a vast crowd beyond man's power to number. They came from every nation and tribe and people and language, and they stood before the throne of the Lamb, dressed in white robes with palm branches in their hands. With a great voice they shouted these words: 'Salvation belongs to our God who sits upon the throne and to the Lamb!'" Revelation 7:4, 9-10.

6 | Jesus, Israel's Salvation

Chapter 7 is the Church's assurance that God's awe-full wrath will not fall on believers. God's people, spiritual Israel, are certified as His own by the seal of the living God who will protect them and fulfill His purposes in their lives.

John's vision depicts the restraining power of the angel from the east, who is given authority to limit the destructive power of God's judgments, and who announced that Israel would be sealed. This angel from the east is a representative of Jesus. Jesus is described in Zechariah's song as the rising sun from heaven who guides feet *"into the path of peace,"* (Luke 1:78-79).

Who are the 144,000 who are sealed? They represent first of all the people of Israel, the full representation of the twelve tribes who historically and spiritually were elected to be God's chosen people. The totality of Israel's elect is suggested by the number 144,000, or 12 x 12,000, which encompasses the full number of the elect from each of the twelve tribes. These are those of whom Paul wrote: *"And so all Israel will be saved, as it is written: 'The deliverer will come from Zion; he will turn godlessness away from Jacob,'"* Romans 11:26.

Also included among the 144,000 are Gentiles, who as wild olive branches have been grafted in the Church. But they do not support the root (Israel), but are supported by the root, Romans 11:18. Elsewhere Paul wrote that salvation is *"first for the Jew, then for the Gentile,"* Romans 1:16. Though Gentiles are included in the 144,000, the climax of God's sealing of the 144,000 will occur when God *"will pour out on the house of David and the inhabitants of Jerusalem a spirit of grace and supplication,"* Zechariah 12:10. *"On that day a fountain will be opened in the house of David and the inhabitants of Jerusalem, to cleanse them from sin and impurity,"* Zechariah 13:1. *"They will call on my name and I will answer them; I will say, 'They are my people,' and they will say, 'The Lord is our God,'"* Zechariah 13:9b.

How will Zechariah's prophecy concerning Israel be fulfilled even as the angel affirmed in Revelation 7:3? Paul's answer in his letter to the Romans is: *"God's gifts and his call are irrevocable. Just as you who were at one time disobedient to God have now received mercy as a result of their disobedience, so they too have now become disobedient in order that they too may now receive mercy as a result of God's mercy to you. For God has bound all men over to disobedience so that he may have mercy on them all,"* Romans 11:29-32. Paul then concludes Romans 11 with a doxology. After John's description of the sealing of the 144,000, which he heard about in his vision, he too records the words of a doxology, this one given by *"the angels encircling the throne, the Elders and the four living creatures"*: *"Amen! Blessing and glory and wisdom and thanksgiving and honor and power and strength be given to our God for timeless ages!"* Revelation 7:12.

The Jews in the Diaspora, particularly those in Asia Minor to whom the letters to the Seven Churches of Asia were written, needed to hear this message of prophecy and doxology as they faced virulent spiritual and physical foes within and without. They were assured that they were sealed as God's own and that other Jews would also receive the seal of God upon their foreheads. After the angel announced this with a *"loud voice,"* he graphically called the roll of the tribes of Israel. This roll call was capped by *"a vast crowd beyond man's power to number. They came from every nation and tribe and people and language, and they stood before the throne of the Lamb, dressed in white robes with palm branches in their hands. With a great voice they shouted these words: 'Salvation belongs to our God who sits upon the throne and to the Lamb,'"* Revelation 7:9-10. Believers in Asia Minor needed to be certain that in time of trial their salvation was secure because it was from God and the Lamb. Furthermore, they were reminded by one of the Elders that at the time of their entry into the Eternal Kingdom *"...the Lamb who is in the center of the throne will be their shepherd and will lead them to springs of living water. And God will wipe away every tear from their eyes,"* Revelation 7:17. Then Jesus will truly be adored and worshipped as Israel's salvation.

Those persons, who according to Revelation 7 waved the palm branches of victory and who wore the white robes of the elect, were forgiven and made holy, and were from every nation. Paul understood what John saw in his vision as an outworking of God's plan of salvation which was for both Jews and Gentiles. He said in Romans 9:6, *"Not all who are descended from Israel are Israel."* In Romans 10:4 he wrote, *"Christ is the end of the law so that there may be righteousness for every one who believes."* The complete number of the elect, the 144,000, then are all those who *"overcome by the blood of the Lamb",* both Jews and Gentiles.

Those of the Church of Asia Minor, indeed all those in the Church of the ages, were made to understand by John's vision that tribulation is for all believers, what Jesus described in Matthew 24:8 as *"the beginning of birth pains,"* John beheld what the Old Testament prophet Zephaniah prophesied, when he foresaw that after a period of severe suffering a redeemed Israel will be gathered in Zion with converted Gentiles who will worship God in the language of Zion, Zephaniah 3:8-20.

Chapter 7 concludes by one of the Elders answering the question he addressed to John as to who those were whom John saw in his vision dressed in white robes by answering, *"These are those who have come through the great oppression; they have washed their robes and made them white in the blood of the Lamb,"* Revelation 7:14. Then the Elder described how the Lamb who was their shepherd would protect them and provide for all their needs by leading them *"to springs of living water."* Israel's sealing then was a promise to the

Churches in Asia Minor and to the Church of the ages that no matter how great their trials Jesus would be their salvation.

The first verse of chapter 8 describes an ominous silence in John's vision that lasted in Heaven, John said, *"for what seemed to me a half hour."* The foreboding silence was followed by the blowing of a trumpet by an angel. The first, second, third and fourth trumpet blasts heralded an unprecedented time of suffering and testing for the early Church.

There were flare ups of persecution following Domitian's reign; but persecution reached its zenith during the time when Diocletian was emperor, 285-305 A.D. In his role as emperor it is said that he sought the liquidation of the Church. Yet many of his own slaves and servants, and even his own wife and daughter were Christians.

He issued four edicts against Christianity which, among other things, required the destruction of all church buildings and ordered all Christians to offer sacrifices to pagan gods. One of his most ignominious deeds was the destruction by soldiers of an entire town in Asia Minor whose inhabitants were predominately Christian. The town may have been Eumenea in Phrygia.

Does John's vision of the blowing of the first four trumpets give a prophetic picture of what the Church would face, particularly during the rule of Diocletian? It would be reasonable to assume that such was the case. When the angel filled a censer with fire from the altar and hurled it on earth, *"there were thunderings and noises, flashes of lightning and an earthquake."*

God was about to test the Church in order to purify it that one day He might through His Son reward the Church for its patient endurance. In the process, the elements that normally sustain life, namely vegetation, the sea and land waters, were all affected by disaster so as to impose hardship, loss and sorrow. Concerning the most essential life sustainer, water, it is said, *"A third of all the waters turned into wormwood, and many people died because the waters had become bitter,"* Revelation 8:11. Finally, following the blowing of the fourth trumpet, a third of the light of the sun, moon and stars was darkened.

These luminaries were often used by prophets to symbolize leaders. Under Diocletian and other Roman emperors, Church leaders often became martyrs because of their faith in the absolute Lordship of Jesus. The diminishing of light was also a portent of the fall of Roman power described in chapter 9. The catastrophic disintegration of Rome had begun.

No wonder there was silence in Heaven. The awful portent of what was to be revealed left the creatures who surrounded the throne of God and the Lamb in an attitude of utter amazement. They too knew that God does not willfully and without purpose afflict His children. This truth was expressed with such deep conviction by Jeremiah when he wrote, *"Because of the Lord's great love we are not consumed, for his compassions never fail. For men are not cast off by the Lord forever. Though he brings grief, he will show compassion, so great is his unfailing love. For he does not willingly bring affliction or grief to the children of men,"* Lamentations 3:22, 31-33.

In what sense did the compassion of the Lord prevail? Under such emperors as Diocletian and Decius, and to a lesser sense under Domitian in John's day, the Church prospered spiritually. As the Church Father Tertullian wrote, *"The blood of the martyrs is seed."*

Christians, emboldened by their example, became strong in the faith. Despite the loss of some lukewarm members who fell away, new converts were won, including people from the higher classes who became Christians in larger numbers during Diocletian's reign. Indeed, Jesus became Israel's salvation as many were willing to die, rejecting all forms of syncretism that in the name of survival required the worship of pagan gods and emperor worship along side of their worship of God and the Lamb.

The first 8 chapters of *Revelation* focus on Jesus' glory. In chapter 1 we see the glorified Jesus in John's vision of the One *"like a Son of Man"*. This in part was an answer to that petition of Jesus' prayer to the Father recorded in John 17:5, *"Father, glorify me in your presence with the glory I had with you before the world began."* His glory is emblazoned in the worship accorded God and the Lamb as described in Revelation 4,5. The Lord of the Church, as Jesus is presented in Revelation 2-3, is also the Lord whose glory is made known to and through His faithful followers who show themselves *"faithful unto death"* during times of great tribulation, as described in Revelation 6-8. Already, through their faithful worship the petition of Jesus' prayer to the Father as recorded in John 17:24 has been partly answered: *"Father, I want those you have given me to be with me where I am, and to see my glory, the glory you have given me because you loved me before the creation of the world."*

Even in chapter 6, which describes John's vision of the breaking of the six seals, God's glory is emphasized in the prayer of the martyrs who confidently worship their Sovereign Lord with the words, *"How long shall it be, O Lord of all, holy and true, before Thou shalt judge and avenge our blood upon the inhabitants of the earth?"* Revelation 6:10.

In chapter 7 God is described as the "shelter" of His people, and the Lamb in the center of the throne as *"their shepherd"*. Chapter 8 speaks of the *"smoke of incense"* *"mingled with the prayers of the saints"*. The four judgments of chapter 8 conclude the section of Revelation which focuses on the glory of God and Jesus, the Lamb. They follow God's trumpet calls to repentance sounded by the angels and are in response to the prayers of the saints. Because the calls were not heeded by Rome, the fall of the city followed as indicated in Revelation 9.

SECTION II: HONOR
Victory For His Beloved City

Biblical Background for: Jesus, Rome's Conqueror
Revelation 9

Key Verses

"Then out of the smoke emerged locusts to descend upon the earth. They were given powers like those of earthly scorpions. They had orders to do no harm to any grass, green thing or tree upon the earth, but to injure only those human beings who did not bear the seal of God upon their foreheads. ...They have tails and stings like scorpions, and it is in their tails that they possess the power to injure men for five months. They have as their king the angel of the pit, whose name in Hebrew is Abaddon and in the Greek Apollyon (meaning the Destroyer),"
Revelation 9:3-4, 10-11.

7 | Jesus, Rome's Conqueror

Chapter 9 of Revelation, which begins with the blowing of the fifth trumpet, depicts the destruction of Rome by the barbarians as the work of Satan himself and his demons. The word barbarian is of Greek origin. The term was applicable to all who did not speak Greek, which was a sign they did not measure up to Hellenic civilization. The victims were those persons *"who did not bear the seal of God upon their foreheads,"* verse 4.

Christians were spared destruction by the barbarians because Christians soon reached an understanding with them, seeing them as instruments of God's judgment. The barbarians have been blamed for destroying the glory of Greek culture and the grandeur of once proud Rome. However, Rome was ripe for destruction because of its economic, social and political problems, accentuated by her moral depravity. The fury of the barbarian forces that caused such chaos and suffering was fueled by Satanic forces which showed no pity for an empire already besotted by moral degradation.

The mystery of God's working in history unfolds as many of the barbarians, whom God permitted Satan to use as instruments of judgment upon Rome, became converts to Christianity. An example of the outworking of God's purposes, as it pertains to the survival and growth of the Church, is seen in negotiations between Pope Gregory the Great and the invading Lombards, which later opened the way for the conversion of many barbarians to orthodox Christianity.

Who in the Seven Churches of Asia under John's care could ever have imagined that less than 500 years later, in the year 476 A.D., the Goths under Odovacar would depose the last Roman emperor, Romulus Augustus. Yet for those who had ears to hear what Jesus, the Lord of the Church, was saying through John's visions, that prospect was certain in God's time.

The announcement was made ironically by an eagle. Rome had paraded its authority, monarchial power and royal splendor under the banner of the eagle; but in John's vision the eagle is a symbol of God's care and strength, as celebrated in the Song of Moses, which tells of God's care of Israel as an eagle cares for its young: *"In a desert land he found him, in a barren and howling waste. He shielded him and cared for him; he guarded him as the apple of his eye, like an eagle that stirs up its nest and hovers over its young, that spreads its wings to catch them and carries them on its pinions,"* Deuteronomy 32:10-11.

It seems entirely fitting that the eagle later became the symbol of John, for in his Gospel his understanding and spiritual contemplation of the divine nature of Jesus soars upward to the heavens like the eagle.

John's vision in chapter 9 gave assurance that Rome one day would fall. The imagery pictured the barbarians as voracious, systematic, effective, disruptive tormentors, cruel in their destructive assault on Rome. They just did not go away.

Barbarian tribes from Germany began to menace the empire in the 200's, but the beginning of the end of the Roman Empire did not occur until the Vandal horde sacked Rome in 455 A.D. During that period decadent Rome retreated, accommodated, and by every device available sought to delay the inevitable. Though not cultured, the foe was intelligent.

Rome's fall was delayed in part due to the proclivity of the invaders to indulge in new found power and wealth until they became soft due to their self-indulgence. Instead of ruling, they often were assimilated.

Hear now the story of Rome's fall as told in John's vision. The star, the symbol of guidance, showed the way to the "fathomless pit," a symbol of despair. Smoke that concealed now poured out, and the pervasive and voracious locusts came forth not to destroy, but to torture. Their target was not verdant grasses or growing trees, but people who had not allowed themselves to be affirmed by God through the imposition of His seal. Death eludes the tortured whose only surcease was that of a shortened year.

The destroyer angel of the place of darkness and despair, who was king of the Abyss, and who variously was known as Abaddon and Apollyon, directed the locusts' activities against those who were targets of the first woe.

The dominance of these creatures of torture was evident in their appearance and the sound of their presence. They wore crowns of gold, bore the intelligence of human beings, and were protected by breastplates like iron. Their presence was like the thunder of many horses and chariots running headlong into battle, and their scorpion tails brought a torment that lasted for five months.

Was this all? No, the first disaster was past, but now the second woe was introduced when the sixth trumpet blew and John saw horsemen whose breastplates gleamed with fiery red, dark blue and sulfur yellow. Horses' heads resembled the heads of lions, and one third of the human race was killed by the fire, smoke and sulfur that came out of their mouths. The tails of the horses were like snakes having heads that inflicted injury.

What John saw in his vision of the horses and their riders was similar to the monsters of pagan mythology. Jesus was impressing on him and the Church that God uses even the fiercest of demonic characters to wreak punishment on those who are foes of the Church, in this case the Roman Empire. A date in history that will always be remembered is August 24, 410 A.D., when the Goths under Alaric stormed the walls of Rome in a surprise attack and pillaged the city for three days. Now for the first time in 800 years Rome had been taken by a foreign enemy.

The imagery in John's vision related to the sack of Rome is powerful in that it draws on Israel's past. The sixth trumpet draws a demonic foe from the Euphrates.

Beyond the Euphrates were the Babylonian and Assyrian Empires, which had been instruments of God's judgment unleashed against disobedient Israel. Now even more terrifying forces would be instruments of judgment used against the great persecutor of the Church, Rome.

The force that would bring about Rome's downfall would be a number that would defy resistance, namely, *"two myriads of two myriads"*, or, as often translated, 200 million. The large number is used to emphasize its indomitable character. One is reminded of the description of the forces God uses to scatter the foes of His people, as found in Psalm 68:17: *"The chariots of God are tens of thousands and thousands of thousands."*

Though Rome was psychologically devastated by her defeat, did her people repent and turn from their wicked ways? No, the worship of the pantheon and occult practices continued. Colonnaded shrines and images continued to be a cover-up for evil practices in Rome. Instead of repentance, the following indictment is spelled out in Revelation 9:20-21: *"The rest of mankind, who did not die in this fearful destruction, neither repented of the works of their own hands nor ceased to worship evil powers and idols of gold, silver, brass, stone, or wood, which can neither see nor hear nor move. Neither did they repent of their murders, their sorceries, their sexual sins, nor of their thieving."* These words are a death knell for all who oppose Jesus, the Lord of the Church, for the loud cry of the eagle in Revelation 8:13 is echoed in every culture in which God's call to repentance is not heeded. The words, *"Alas, alas, alas for the inhabitants of the earth,"* reverberate as we see through John's eyes the *"solitary eagle flying in midheaven."* The power of Jesus is greater than the power of Rome. Therefore, Paul wrote in the first chapter of his epistle to the Romans verse 18, *"The wrath of God is being revealed from heaven against all the godlessness and wickedness of men who suppress the truth by their wicked-*

ness." But the good news of Jesus Christ, he said, *"is the power of God for the salvation of everyone who believes,"* Romans 1:16.

So beginning with chapter 9 and continuing through 20:10, *Revelation* focuses on the honor of God as Jesus exercises dominion over the forces of evil. Through the exercise of dominion Jesus, too, is given honor by the Church. Wrath for the wicked and salvation for the believer is the basis for the honor Jesus receives.

Biblical Background for: Jesus, The King
Revelation 10 and 11

Key Verse

"The seventh angel blew his trumpet. There arose loud voices in Heaven and they were saying, 'The Kingship of the world now belongs to our Lord and to his Christ, and he shall be king for timeless ages!'"
Revelation 11:15.

8 | Jesus, The King

John learned through his visions of the *"little book"* and the *"two witnesses"* that the faithful proclamation of God's Word would result in loud voices declaring, *"The kingship of the world now belongs to our Lord and to his Christ, and he shall be king for timeless ages,"* Revelation 11:15.

Chapters 10 and 11 mark a definite transition in the *Revelation* of Jesus through the visions John received. John himself is no longer primarily an observer. He is now, more than ever before, a participator in the Church's proclamation of the good news of the Kingdom. The little book itself which John ingested contained the rest of the visions of *Revelation*; for upon eating it he was told, *"It is again your duty to prophesy about many peoples, nations, languages and kings,"* Revelation 10:11.

John's personal preparation for the proclamation of good news pertaining to the end times is suggested by verse 4 of chapter 10, *"When the seven thunders had rolled I was on the point of writing but I heard a voice from Heaven saying, 'Seal up what the seven thunders said, but do not write it down!'"* This may suggest that what the seven thunders said was for his own information and inspiration, in light of his great task of prophesying.

The universal scope of his message was dramatized when he *"saw another mighty angel descending from Heaven. He was clothed in a cloud, and there was a rainbow around his head. His face blazed like the sun, his legs like pillars of fire, and he had a little book lying open in his hand. He planted his right foot on the sea and his left foot on the land,..."* Revelation 10:1-2.

Beginning in verse 5 it says concerning this same angel, *"Then the angel whom I had seen bestriding the sea and the land raised his right hand to Heaven and swore by the living one of timeless ages, who created Heaven, earth and sea and all that is in them: 'There shall be no more delay!'"* Revelation 10:5-6.

The destruction of Rome described in chapter 9 was a prelude to the final accomplishment of God's redemptive purposes. Until that part of God's agenda in history was completed, the redemptive events associated with the last time, referred to in 10:7 as *"the mysterious purpose of God,"* were delayed. *The "living one of the timeless ages"* stood behind the promise that the trumpet blast of the seventh angel would precede the completion of *"the mysterious purpose of God"*.

Meanwhile, John's role in the delivery of the prophetic Word was symbolized by his eating the *"little book"*. He was told that the result for him would be both sweet and bitter. The taste was sweet in John's mouth, because God's Word brings life and joy. But at the same time it was bitter in John's stomach, because God's purposes are not fulfilled without the experience of sorrow and destruction in the lives of those who hear the Word of God but respond with acts of obdurate disobedience.

By John's example we learn that the Church's task is to proclaim the good news of Jesus, the coming king, regardless of the consequences, because He has given to the Church the promise of Matthew 24:14, *"And this gospel of the kingdom will be preached in the whole world as a testimony to all nations, and then the end will come."*

Jesus had said to Peter concerning John, *"If I want him to remain alive until I return, what is that to you? You must follow me,"* John 21:22.

In a very real sense Jesus, the glorified Son of Man, the Lord of the Church, returned to John on Patmos with the urgent message to proclaim to all nations the Gospel of the Kingdom over which He reigns as king.

What John was told to do and not to do in the first two verses of chapter 11 tells us what God's plan for the Church is during the last days leading up to the King's return, when Jesus will come to take the Church as His Bride. The Temple in John's vision is seen as a material representation of the Church.

As in II Samuel 8:2, in which David's measurements determined the issue of life and death, so the measuring of the Temple mentioned in Revelation 11:1-2 has to do with an issue of very great significance.

What would endure and what would not according to John's measurement? The very core of the Church, represented by the altar and the area where worshippers gather, will endure persecution. But John was told that there would be no point in measuring the outer court, for its identity was with those outside the Church, persons from many nations who, for a period of limited duration, represented by forty–two months, would make life very difficult for the Church; but their effort to destroy the Church would fail. Even so, the animal, an evil beast which John saw emerging from the pit, would create havoc for the Church.

What havoc would the animal create in its destructive foray? The beastly creature which is the epitome of all that is contrary to the Kingdom of God killed the two witnesses. Who were the witnesses? Understood in terms of the symbolism in John's vision, they are representatives of the Church.

In chapter 1 the lampstand is the Church. In 11:4 the two lampstands are the Church of the Old Testament and the Church of the New Testament. The two witnesses are lamps that shine forth from the lampstands. The lamps have Elijah-like *"power to shut up the sky and stop any rain from falling,"* Revelation 11:6a. The lamps are able to exercise this power through prayer: *"The prayer of a righteous man is powerful and effective,"* James 5:16.

James in the next verse associates the power of prayer with Elijah's ability to prevent rain, as recorded in I Kings 17:1. The

Church (lampstands) also hold lamps with Moses-like qualities. They *"have power to turn the waters into blood, and to strike the earth with any plague as often as they wish,"* Revelation 11:6b, (Exodus 7-12).

Is this not John's way of describing the power of the Church's message, even as Paul wrote to the Corinthians, *"For we are to God the aroma of Christ among those who are being saved and those who are perishing. To the one we are the smell of death; to the other, the fragrance of life,"* II Corinthians 2:15-16a. Moses, God's spokesman, called down plagues upon the Egyptians, but even some of the Egyptians became believers in Israel's God and joined the Israelites in the Exodus, Exodus 12:38. Likewise, after the two witnesses received *"the Spirit of life from God"* and *"went up to Heaven,"* God's judgment occurred; but terrified survivors *"acknowledged the glory of the God of Heaven,"* Revelation 11:11-13.

The Moses and Elijah qualities of the Church we find in New Testament characters like Stephen and John the Baptist, whose bodies lay exposed following martyrdom. John the Baptist came alive in Jesus, who was viewed by some as the embodiment of John. Who can doubt but that Stephen came alive in Paul, who consented in Stephen's martyrdom: the same Paul who later in the spirit of the martyr fearlessly proclaimed the Gospel, up until the time when he himself became a victim of Rome's attempt to stamp out Christianity.

Persons like Elijah and Moses under the Old Covenant, and like John the Baptist and Stephen under the New Covenant, were lamps in the Church. Concerning John the Baptist Jesus said, *"John was a lamp that burned and gave light, and you chose for a time to enjoy his light."* John 5:35. Luke wrote concerning Stephen, *"Now Stephen, a man full of God's grace and power, did great wonders and miraculous signs among the people. Opposition arose, however, ..."* Acts 6:8-9.

John's vision was an assurance that others like John the Baptist, Stephen, and yes, King Asa of Judah, I Kings 15:4, II Chronicles 14:1-2, would continue to be shining lamps in the Church of the future.

What would make them faithful and effective leaders in the face of the blandishments and terror of the forces of evil? The answer to the Church of John's day and ours is in the symbolism of the olive trees in John's vision. The two olive trees represented the Jewish and Gentile Church of John's day and the future. Paul in Romans 11 refers to the Jewish Church as the cultivated olive tree and the Gentile Church as the wild olive tree.

The angel in John's vision was saying that through the power of the Holy Spirit represented by the oil in the olive tree, the Church (lampstands) would send witnesses (lamps) into the world to glorify King Jesus, the Light of the World.

Despite martyrdoms resulting from persecution fomented by the forces of darkness, the true Church would continue its faithful witness in the world.

If there was any question in the minds of the Christians living in the Province of Asia in John's day as to the final outcome in the struggle between the forces of good and evil, the Church and Rome, those concerns would be allayed by God's actions in John's vision, as described in 11:11-13.

As a result of divine intervention, the celebration and partying on the part of those who gloated over the sight of the dead bodies of the witnesses in the street, which were exposed to scavengers and the jeers of those who denied them the decency of burial, was short lived (three and one–half days). The heavenly homecoming of the witnesses was accompanied by a trumpet blast and the loud voices of the hosts of heaven, who sang praises to the King and worshipped God, as described in 11:15-18.

Also in John's vision we are made aware of a stark contrast between the Jerusalem following our Lord's crucifixion, *"which is called by those with spiritual understanding Sodom and Egypt,"* Revelation 11:8, places of apostasy, corruption and godless idolatry; and the glimpse of the New Jerusalem, the *"Temple of God in Heaven,"* described in 11:19 as a sight which John saw accompanied by nature's salute. *"The ark of his agreement,"* no longer in earthly Jerusalem, once the great city of David, is now the ark of God's covenant in the Temple of the heavenly Jerusalem. The New Jerusalem, which John in chapter 21 saw *"descending from God out of Heaven,"* was a fulfillment of God's intention as expressed in I Kings 11:36: *"I will give one tribe to his son (Rehoboam) so that David my servant will always have a lamp before me in Jerusalem, the city where I chose to put my*

Name." The same thought is expressed in II Kings 8:19, *"He (God) had promised to maintain a lamp for David and his descendants forever."* That lamp, *"God's message and borne witness to Jesus,"* 1:9, will have as its final destiny the New Jerusalem.

By his vision of the ark of the agreement in Heaven, John was assured of the truth expressed by "loud voices in Heaven": *"The kingship of the world now belongs to our Lord and to his Christ, and he shall be king for timeless ages,"* Revelation 11:15.

Because we are children of God through faith in Jesus Christ, the gift of the Kingdom of God which is *"righteousness, peace and joy in the Holy Spirit,"* Romans 14:17, is the result of our covenant relationship with King Jesus. Therefore, during our earthly sojourn, even though the *"holy city"*, the Church of Christ, may be trampled upon by its tormentors for forty–two months, it is certain that even during those periods of hardship there will be a humble, faithful Church witness covering the same period of time as indicated by 1,260 days, 11:2-3.

King Jesus continues to give to the Church threatened by apostasy and immorality the authority to reign with Him, even as He did to the Church in Thyatira: *"To the one who is victorious, who carries out my work to the end, I will give authority over the nations, just as I myself have received authority from my Father, and I will give him the morning star. He shall 'shepherd them with a rod of iron'; he shall 'dash them in pieces like a potter's vessel,'"* Revelation 2:26-27.

Biblical Background for: Jesus, The Lamb Slain
Revelation 12

Key Verses

"Then I heard a great voice in Heaven cry: 'Now the salvation of the power and kingdom of our God, and the authority of his Christ, have come! For the accuser of our brethren has been thrown down from his place, where he stood before our God accusing them day and night. Now they have conquered him through the blood of the Lamb, and through the Word to which they bore witness. They did not cherish life even in the face of death,'" Revelation 12:10-11.

9 | Jesus, The Lamb Slain

The question that is answered in chapter 12 is, "Who is in control—the evil one or God?" A woman, a child and the earth combine to answer, "God". The outcome on earth was determined by what happened in heaven, 12:7-9. The victorious Lamb in 12:11 who was slain is, to use Jacques Ellul's metaphor, the silhouette of Jesus Christ. Throughout *Revelation* that silhouette is ever visible to those who have spiritual eyes to see. He is none other than the *"Lamb slain from the foundation of the world,"* to whom the book of life belongs, (Revelation 13:8).

Even though the evil one accuses them day and night, the Church was seen in John's vision as overcomers *"through the blood of the Lamb, and through the Word to which they bore witness,"* Revelation 12:11. Therefore, the huge dragon, Satan, was unable to unsettle the followers of the Lord who had no fear of death.

How does the blood of the Lamb hold God's children steady, even when the powers of evil are unleashed in all their fury? Before answering that question, Jesus permitted John to see in his vision an enormous red dragon *"with seven heads and ten horns, with a diadem upon each of his heads. His tail swept down a third of the stars in the sky and hurled them upon the earth,"* Revelation 12:3-4. The crowns represented Satan's rule over the unredeemed world, which Paul described in Colossians 1:13 as *"the dominion of darkness"*. The horns represented the destructive power of the dragon. Verse nine in this chapter indicates that the stars referred to in verse four are the angels who fell with Satan, the one whom Jesus saw *"fall like lightning from heaven,"* Luke 10:18.

Jesus said, in Luke 10:20, to the seventy–two who returned from their mission that they should rejoice, not because of their share in His victory over the powers of evil, but rather in the fact *"that your names are written in heaven."*

The Lamb is the one to whom the book of life belongs which contains the names of the redeemed. The story of how one's name is included in the book of life points to a victory achieved by the Lamb that gives steadiness to God's people, even in the worst of times.

The story told in Revelation 12, which had its beginning in Heaven, is one that should be told again and again.

John saw in his vision that his persecuted brothers in the faith were overcomers through the blood of the Lamb. Even so, John was told that they would be facing more severe testings in the near future, because the devil knew his time was short.

The loud voice from Heaven in John's vision reminded him of those in the past who were faithful, because they did not cherish their lives in the face of death, but rather were willing to surrender physical life for eternal life which Jesus promised the faithful in John 12:25.

Their overcoming was possible not only because of the redeeming blood of the Lamb, but also because of their faithfulness in serving Jesus, John 12:26. That service is described here in Revelation 12 as grounded in *"the Word to which they bore witness."* The victory of the Lamb and the Church's faithfulness in bearing witness to the Word keeps God's children steady in the face of persecution.

Revelation 12 focuses on something entirely new that happened when a woman of creation became the mother of Jesus. Let's review the story of the outworking of God's redemptive plan as told in John's vision.

In John's vision Mary, the mother of Jesus, reflected the radiance of the sun, gained dominion over darkness (the moon was at her feet), and in effect became the one responsible for the apostolic leadership of the Church (a crown of twelve stars was upon her head), all because she gave birth to the Christ, *"who is God over all forever praised!"* Romans 9:5.

Before the birth of this God-Man, the dragon stood in front of the pregnant woman that He might be devoured at the moment of birth; but the dragon's henchman, Herod, did not succeed in destroying Him. Instead, the Father said concerning His Son, *"You will rule them with an iron scepter; you will dash them to pieces like pottery,"* Psalm 2:9. This aspect of the *"sign"* given John is also alluded to in 12:5.

Beginning with verse 13 the woman in John's vision took the form of the Church. The Church *"was given two great eagle's wings so that she could fly to her place in the desert, where she is kept safe from the serpent for a time and times and half a time,"* Revelation 12:14. This word concerning how God will protect His Church is no doubt an allusion to Exodus 19:4, *"You yourselves have seen what I did to Egypt and how I carried you on eagles' wings and brought you to myself."*

The Church would be sustained, as God's people were sustained during the Exodus, by the presence of God in the spiritual desert of this world. Even as Mary was taken care of for an indefinite time until the danger was past and she could return home from Egypt; so the Church will be sustained by God, *"for a time and times and half a time,"* meaning an indefinite time, until the day when creation will absorb the torrent of evil directed by the dragon against the Church. Through the cross and empty tomb God's will was done on earth as in Heaven. Thus the Almighty One thwarted the effort of the dragon to destroy the Church. However, the defeated dragon still makes war against the spiritual offspring of the Church—*"those who obey the commandments of God and bear their witness to Jesus,"* Revelation 12:17.

The Seven Churches of Asia and their spiritual offspring can take comfort in knowing that the fury of Satan is due to their faithfulness, which will be rewarded. The retelling of the story of redemption is the testimony that will energize and rekindle the faith of the Church that will conquer through the redeeming power of the Lamb slain.

Because of the life, work, death and resurrection of Jesus, the Lamb slain, *"we are more than conquerors through him who loved us,"* Romans 8:37. Therefore, we can declare with Paul, *"If God is for us, who can be against us?"* Romans 8:31.

Biblical Background for: Jesus, God's Enduring Wisdom
Revelation 13

Key Verse

"Understanding is needed here: let every thinking man calculate the number of the animal. It is the number of a man, and its number is six hundred and sixty-six," Revelation 13:18.

10 | Jesus, God's Enduring Wisdom

In chapter 13, the powers of evil are exposed in John's vision. It is important to the Church that the nefarious spiritual nature of evil be fully known. The dragon, Satan, mentioned in 12:3, was seen as *"a huge red dragon with seven heads and ten horns, with a diadem upon each of his heads,"* which designated him as the ultimate expression of evil in charge of a host of allies. Satan uses those allies in ways that best suit his purposes.

Where did the allies of Satan come from? Is the answer found in Revelation 12? After the ascension of Jesus, mentioned in 12:5, which marked the end of His saving work on earth, we learn what John saw in his vision as recorded in Revelation 12:7-9: *"Then war broke out in Heaven. Michael and his angels battled with the dragon. The dragon and his angels fought back, but they did not prevail and they were expelled from Heaven. So the huge dragon, the serpent of ancient times, who is called the devil and Satan, the deceiver of the whole world, was hurled down upon the earth, and his angels were hurled down with him."*

Does the hurling down of Satan the deceiver and his angels reflect what is described in Isaiah 14:11-15 and Ezekiel 28:11-19? No, the fallen Day Star (Lucifer) in Isaiah and primal being in Ezekiel, who dwelt in the Garden of Eden, and whose pride is likened to the King of Tyre, are associated with Satan's fall at the time, when, as recorded in Genesis 3, Adam and Eve were driven from the garden. Their expulsion also marked the beginning of the loss of Lucifer's exalted position.

There is, however, a direct relation between Genesis 3:15, the mother promise, and Revelation 12:9. The fulfillment of the Genesis prophecy pertaining to the cross has made certain the final hurling down (defeat) of Satan. Genesis 3:15 pointed to God's wisdom, the event of the cross which will one day result in the complete defeat of Satan. Concerning that wisdom Paul wrote, *"It is because of him (God) that you are in Christ Jesus, who has become for us wisdom from God—that is, our righteousness, holiness and redemption,"* I Corinthians 1:30.

If 12:9 is not a reflection of the Isaiah and Ezekiel passages, despite the fact that the three passages speak of Satan's humiliation, then what is its point of reference? Because of the redemptive work of Jesus and the victory of His flaming servant Michael, Hebrews 1:7, Satan the accuser no longer has any basis for his accusations against believers.

This, in essence, is the thrust of the Revelation 12:9 passage. Any accusations are no longer valid because, *"Now the salvation of the power and kingdom of our God, and the authority of his Christ, have come!"* Revelation 12:10. Satan's lofty position as an accuser no longer exists, even though he still continues to accuse. Satan's lofty position was nullified when the angel Michael, the defender of God's people, defeated the dragon, figuratively resulting in the deceiver being hurled to earth.

Michael's victory confirmed the victory of the cross, so that now Satan has been deprived of the ability to humiliate a believer by the use of suffocating guilt. Michael, God's ministering spirit, applies the healing balm of God's forgiving love which flows from calvary. Thus Jesus, whom Paul calls *"wisdom from God,"* through the cross has rendered Satan's attempts to malign believers ineffective.

The same deceiver who, as Ezekiel said, was expelled from the garden paradise and the mount of God because it was said of him, *"Your heart became proud on account of your beauty, and you corrupted your wisdom because of your splendor,"* Ezekiel 28:17, was now rendered inept as an accuser by Jesus, the wisdom of God. Therefore, John heard in his vision a loud voice from heaven say, *"Now they have conquered him through the blood of the Lamb, and through the Word to which they bore witness. They did not cherish life even in the face of death!"* Revelation 12:11.

The word to the Churches of Asia and to us is that a faithful witness, even if it means death, will make God's faithful ones conquerors of the dragon. For this victory of Jesus, God's Enduring Wisdom, the Heavens are called on to rejoice, but the earth and the sea can be expected to experience the "great fury" of the devil: *"Therefore, rejoice, O Heavens, and all you who live in the Heavens! But alas for the earth and the sea, for the devil has come down to you in great fury, knowing that his time is short!"* Revelation 12:12.

Because his time is short, Satan will make use of all his allies—in particular the animal from the sea and the animal from the earth. His attacks will be directed against the offspring of the Church, (Revelation 12:17).

John's warning to those *"who keep the commandments of God and bear their witness to Jesus"* is underscored, as in his vision he stood on the sand of the seashore and beheld a beast emerging from the sea. Concerning this animal John wrote, *"... there rose out of the sea before my eyes an animal with seven heads and ten horns. There were diadems upon its horns and blasphemous names upon its heads,"* Revelation 13:1.

To understand this symbolism one must compare what is said in 13:1-10, with a parallel passage in Daniel 7:2-8. In pursuing this comparison, it is evident that the element of persecution obviously underlies both passages and the animal identities are the same; but in *Revelation* the leopard, bear and lion are characteristics of a composite animal, whereas in Daniel they are mentioned separately, one by one.

The composite beast in *Revelation "had the appearance of a leopard,"* suggesting cunningness, while it had strong feet like a bear, and a mouth like a lion, with which it could tear and masticate its victims. As the animals of Daniel represented persecuting governments often ruthless in their treatment of believers, so it would seem that the composite beast of *Revelation* would represent Rome as a combination of the ferocious qualities associated with the empires to which Daniel refers.

Rome here is seen as the embodiment of antichrist. Ironically, in Revelation 17 the forces of antichrist take a different form, representing the self-destructive nature of evil, which a sovereign God exploits by putting it into the hearts of evil doers to destroy Babylon, 17:16-17, which is the citadel of evil representing all in life that is contrary to the New Jerusalem.

The animal from the sea is a mirror of the dragon, from whom he receives his authority. Both have ten horns and seven heads, but the beast has the crowns on his horns, whereas the dragon has the crowns on his heads. This indicates that the role of the beast with crowns on its horns is to maim and destroy. That is its crowning achievement; whereas the dragon rules the kingdom of evil with crowns on its heads, reminding us of the seven heads of Daniel's persecuting empires, Daniel 7:3-7.

The seven heads of the beast represent the seven hills on which Rome was built, 17:9. Latin poets often described Rome in terms of its seven hills. It is evident in chapter 17 that Babylon, spiritually speaking the *"mother of prostitutes,"* relied on the beast with its seven heads in the same way that Rome securely rested upon its seven hills. In Revelation 17:9 we are told that the seven heads of the animal from the sea are also seven kings. When we consider that part of John's vision recorded in chapter 17, we shall attempt to identify those 7 rulers.

The ten horns on the beast, according to 17:12, are ten rulers, some of whom were likely in John's time already a part of the imperial rulership of the Roman Empire. The Roman Empire had ten imperial provinces, which were as follows: Achaia, Africa, Asia, Britain, Egypt, Gaul, Germany, Italy, Spain and Syria. As the empire began to unravel due to moral decay and economic instability, forces of unrest, particularly in the more distant provinces, mounted insurrections which were fanned by attacks by barbarian forces. The number 10 may represent a combination of powers which under the sway of the beast finally brought down the mighty Roman Empire; or 10, as in many places in the Bible, may simply be related to the concept of numerical fullness.

The enemies of Rome in time just became too much for the weakened empire. The morality of those enemy forces was not superior to that of Rome. Remember, Rome's foes were under the dominion of the beast of the sea, representing the governmental allies of the dragon. As such, they had *"blasphemous names"* upon their heads.

Rome already had spelled blasphemy with a capital B. Her emperors demanded homage that amounted to worship. Some of them ordered that they be addressed as *"Lord"* and *"Savior"*. Refusal to do so resulted in death, or the living death of banishment. Very severe persecution of Christians began with Nero, who was emperor, 54-68 A.D. Believers were crucified. Others were burned as torches for the entertainment of the masses.

Reference is made in 13:3 to the wounding of the head of one of the Roman emperors. But the wound that appeared to be mortal had healed. John, who observed the healed wound in his vision, no doubt associated the mortal wound with Nero's suicide in 68 A.D. Possibly the healing that made possible the continuing of Nero's nefarious persecution of the Church was embodied in the person of Domitian, the cruel emperor who had banished John to Patmos. However, I believe it is more likely that Diocletian is the emperor in question. See my comments on pages 64, 124 and 125.

After the depiction of the nature and activities of the first beast, there is a parenthetical word from John to his readers introduced with the words, *"Let the listener hear this: If any man is destined for captivity he will go into captivity. If any man kills with the sword he must himself be killed with the sword. Amid all this stands the endurance and faith of the saints,"* Revelation 13:9-10. John was saying to his readers that they should hold fast to the faith, realizing that their true strength was of an inner spiritual nature.

A second beast, who was subservient to the first, was seen in John's vision emerging from the earth. This animal from the earth represented the kind of wisdom which James, in James 3:15, described as *"earthly, unspiritual, of the devil"*.

His wisdom is humanistic religion and philosophy, which is antichristian. Yet his power and ability to deceive causes persons to bow to the image of the first beast. As the embodiment of worldly wisdom this urbane animal appears lamb-like, but speaks with the awesome authority of the dragon.

In his humanistic disguise the animal from the earth forced the placement of the mark of the animal of the sea on the hands (deeds) or the foreheads (minds) of those who came under its spell. This mark empowered all the *"small and great, rich and poor, free men and slaves,"* Revelation 13:16, giving them the exclusive right to buy and sell. The number of the animal from the sea, with which many felt compelled to identify, is the number of man raised to the highest level, 666. The humanistic animal of earth deceived them into believing that they could reach the height of man's greatest fulfillment by accepting completely the humanistic wisdom, with which he, the false prophet, 16:13, 19:20, enticed them to bow down to the image of the monstrous first animal, which is worldly government, the very embodiment of antichrist.

John had sensed that this spirit of antichrist was present in his day when he wrote, *"Dear children, this is the last hour; and as you have heard that the antichrist is coming even now many antichrists have come. This is how we know it is the last hour. They went out from us, but they did not really belong to us. For if they had belonged to us, they would have remained with us; but their going showed that none of them belonged to us,"* I John 2:18-19.

Before John was banished to Patmos it was evident that the spirit of antichrist was already at work, deluding "almost" Christians into thinking that humanistic byways are essential to fulfillment. Evidence of this *"falling away"* is also present in the letters to the Seven Churches of Asia in Revelation 2 and 3. Now in John's vision of antichrist in Revelation 13, he is made aware that those whose names are not written in the book of life belonging to the Lamb will worship the beast, 13:8.

Though the Roman hegemony of John's day brought many benefits to its subjects in terms of cultural and economic advantages, it was not without a spiritual price. The demands of the Roman emperors often required a commitment of body and spirit that only is due the Lord and His Christ. The Church needed to be warned that the empire, which could be beneficient, would also be bestial if its demands were not met. The subtle nature of evil needs to be guarded against during periods of relative calm, as well as during times of overt hostility.

The seductive spirit of antichrist and the false prophet is hard at work in our day seeking to deceive even the elect. In the novel by Frank E. Peretti entitled, *This Present Darkness*, Bernice learned "from the diary of her sister, Pat," the nature of the evil that led to her self-inflicted death. In a letter Pat wrote to an evil spirit she called "Thomas", which is included in her diary, Bernice sensed that, *"Pat wrote in a style of someone under a very strange, lofty-sounding delusion,"* p. 315. Bernice's friend Susan, who passed the diary on to her, said concerning evil spirit entities, *"To the atheistic scientists, they might appear as extraterrestrials, often with their own spaceships; to evolutionists they might claim to be highly evolved beings; to the lonely, they might appear as long-lost relatives speaking from the other side of the grave; Jungian psychologists consider them 'archetypal images' dredged from the collective consciousness of the human race. Hey, listen, whatever description or definition fits, whatever shape, whatever form it takes to win a person's confidence and appeal to his vanity, that's the form they take. And they tell the deluded seeker of truth whatever he or she wants to hear until they finally have that person in their complete control,"* p. 314.

How are the followers of Jesus, God's Enduring Wisdom, expected to deal with the powers of evil? Is it acceptable for those opposed to abortion to kill those who perform abortions? Should a Christian militantly lash out by physically harming evil-doers? The answer to both questions is "no". In Jude, verse 9, it reads, *"But even the archangel Michael, when he was disputing with the devil about the body of Moses, did not dare to bring a slanderous accusation against him, but said, 'The Lord rebuke you!'"*

After John's vision of the animal from the sea he wrote, *"This calls for patient endurance and faithfulness on the part of the saints,"* Revelation 13:10 NIV. After John's vision of the animal from the earth he wrote, *"This calls for wisdom. If anyone has insight, let him calculate the number of the beast, for it is man's number. His number is 666,"* Revelation 13:18 NIV.

In a word, the Christian must learn and practice the ways of Jesus, God's Enduring Wisdom, described by James: *"But the wisdom that comes from heaven is first of all pure; then peace loving, considerate, submissive, full of mercy and good fruit, impartial and sincere. Peacemakers who sow in peace raise a harvest of righteousness,"* James 3:17-18.

Only when Christians live in the spirit of this wisdom from heaven will the world see in us Jesus, God's Enduring Wisdom, whose life and deeds are antithetical to the "wisdom" of antichrist and the false prophet.

As the Church at Pergamum was enticed by the teachings of Balaam and the Nicolaitans, so the Church today must beware of teachings antithetical to the Christian faith.

In the words of Jude we are *"to contend for the faith that was once for all entrusted to the saints,"* verse 3. To do this we need to heed the admonition of Jude: *"But you, dear friends, build yourselves up in your most holy faith and pray in the Holy Spirit,"* verse 20.

Biblical Background for: Jesus, The Giver Of A New Song
Revelation 14

Key Verses

"Then I looked again and before my eyes the Lamb was standing on Mount Sion, and with him were a hundred and forty-four thousand who had his name and his Father's name written upon their foreheads. Then I heard a sound coming from Heaven like the roar of a great waterfall and the heavy rolling of thunder. Yet the sound which I heard was also like the music of harpists sweeping their strings. And now they are singing a new song of praise before the throne, and before the four living creatures and the Elders. No one could learn that song except the one hundred and forty-four thousand who had been redeemed from the earth,"
Revelation 14:1-3.

11 | Jesus, The Giver Of A New Song

Following the visions of evil entities in chapter 13 John is given the visions recorded in chapter 14, which are meant to fortify spiritually the strength of Christians. The full number of the elect, represented by the number 144,000, composed of both Jews and Gentiles are sealed by having the name of the Lamb and His Father on their foreheads. Standing beside the 144,000 is the Lamb who is with them on Mount Zion, the location of the New Jerusalem, His blameless body, the Church.

His beloved Holy City, the New Jerusalem, is God's dwelling place, 21:1-3. Sealed by the name of God and the Lamb written on their foreheads, the 144,000 *"are singing a new song of praise before the throne,"* Revelation 14:3. Because they are undefiled and purchased by the Lamb, they are offered as *"first fruits to God and to the Lamb."* Their offering of praise and worship *"before the four living creatures and the Elders"* is accompanied by a sound *"like the music of harpists sweeping their strings."*

How reassuring this vision of John is to those facing the powers of evil! They see themselves as one day occupying the throne room first described in chapter 4. They are the same persons described in 7:14: *"These are those who have come through the great oppression; they have washed their robes and made them white in the blood of the Lamb."* Of them it is said in 14:5, *"They have never been guilty of any falsehood; they are beyond reproach."* This can be said of them because of the sacrifice of the Lamb; for it is written in Hebrews 10:14,17, *"because by one sacrifice he has made perfect forever those who are being made holy. Then he adds: 'Their sins and lawless acts I will remember no more.'"* No wonder it was said of the 144,000, *"No one could learn that song except the 144,000 who had been redeemed from the earth,"* for Jesus had given them a new song.

Knowing this day is coming the Church of John's day and ours ought to heed the words of Colossians 3:15-16: *"Let the peace of Christ rule in your hearts, since as members of one body you were called to peace. And be thankful. Let the word of Christ dwell in you richly as you teach and admonish one another with all wisdom, and as you sing psalms, hymns and spiritual songs with gratitude in your hearts to God."*

After seeing the vision of the Lamb and the 144,000, as described in the first 5 verses of chapter 14, John has a new vision described in verses 6-13. It is introduced with the words, *"Then I saw another angel flying in midheaven, holding the everlasting Gospel to proclaim to the inhabitants of the earth—to every nation and tribe and language and people,"* Revelation 14:6.

Before the time comes described in the first vision of chapter 14, the Church must faithfully do what the angel in John's vision is seen doing, namely, proclaim the everlasting Gospel to all in the awareness that then the end will come, Matthew 24:14. The urgency of that task is further emphasized by Jesus in Matthew 24:24, *"For false Christs and false prophets will appear and perform great signs and miracles to deceive even the elect - if that were possible."*

The message of the first angel who warns of judgment is, *"Reverence God, and give glory to him; for the hour of his judgment has come! Worship him who made Heaven and earth, the sea and the springs of water,"* Revelation 14:7.

The wording of the angel's message is reminiscent of the urgency of proclamation emphasized by Jesus in Luke 17:26-27, *"Just as it was in the days of Noah, so also will it be in the days of the Son of Man. People were eating, drinking, marrying and being given in marriage up to the day Noah entered the ark. Then the flood came and destroyed them all."* The sense of the urgency of proclamation was important in John's day and is even more so in our day.

The second angel emphasized the certainty of Babylon's fall as if it had already occurred. The angel cried, *"Fallen, fallen is Babylon the great! She who made all nations drink the wine of her passionate unfaithfulness!"* Revelation 14:8. While Babylon could refer to all the powers of evil as symbolized by Old Testament Babylon so vividly described in Isaiah 47, it would seem more likely that here it is a cryptic reference to Rome.

It appears to have been previously so used in I Peter 5:13. Peter's veiled reference to Rome may have been used to protect both the Roman church and Peter from the wrath of Emperor Nero.

John's usage of Babylon as a coded word for Rome here in chapter 14 may have been the angel's way of protecting him and the Churches of Asia from a greater expression of persecution under Emperor Domitian. However, though the word Babylon in 14:8 is a coded word related to the prophetic description of Rome's fall in chapter 9, it is also likely used as a transitional word pointing to its broader usage in chapters 16, 17 and 18.

Babylon in those chapters is used in connection not only with the fall of Rome, but also in reference to the destruction of all the opponents of the heavenly Jerusalem, the city of the living God, which Hebrews 12:22-24 identifies as the Church, and the spiritual entities which define and support the Church. What a boost for the faith of John, the Seven Churches of Asia, and the Church of the ages this prophetic announcement of Babylon's fall provides. It adds power and lustre to the *"new song"* sung by the 144,000.

This broader understanding of the word Babylon is given credence by the words of the third angel in John's third vision recorded in chapter 14. Verses 9-11 underscore the truth that *"the way of the transgressor is hard."* The wrath of God will fall on all who worship the animal and its statue, and on all those who have accepted its mark of ownership. The vivid description of verse 11 is indeed a strong warning to those tempted to receive the mark of the animal's name.

Following this third vision is another one of John's admonitions: *"This calls for patient endurance on the part of the saints who obey God's commandments and remain faithful to Jesus,"* Revelation 14:12 NIV. This admonition is followed by words spoken by a voice from Heaven which also give more power and lustre to the *"new song"* of the 144,000:

"Write this! From henceforth happy are the dead who die in the Lord!"

"Happy indeed," says the Spirit, *"for they rest from their labors and their deeds go with them!"* Revelation 14:13.

The latter part of verse 13, which speaks of those *"who die in the Lord"* is less ambiguous in Phillips than in either the NIV or RSV translations. The New English Bible labors for even greater clarity in its translation, *"for they take with them the record of their deeds."* How comforting the words of verse 13 must have been to believers in John's day who faced the prospect of severe persecution and the possibility of death! This benediction would fortify their faith as they faced whatever the future held. The same may be said of us today.

Following John's vision of the angel of Gospel proclamation, and the cry of the angel announcing the doom of Babylon, and the loud crying of the angel spelling out the dire consequences of judgment upon the worshippers of the beast, three other angels combine to announce the blood letting that would accompany the thrusting of the sharp sickle of God's wrath into the clusters of grapes. Another angel called upon the angel with a golden crown on his head, who was *"sitting upon the cloud with the appearance of a man,"* to reap with his sharp sickle the clusters of ripe grapes.

The one *"with the appearance of a man"* is actually the Son of Man, Jesus. In fact, most translations make that clear because the word *"son"* is in the Greek text. The overall picture in 14:14-20 is one of both salvation and judgment, and the setting is both historical and liturgical.

The city mentioned in verse 20 is Jerusalem. In the same verse mention is made of the flowing of blood outside the city. Jesus Himself was thrown into the winepress of God's wrath; and His blood, figuratively speaking, rose as high as horses' bridles over all of creation.

Creation is represented by the figure 1600 stadia, mentioned in the NIV. What a fitting depiction of creation! Four is the number of creation. All of creation then becomes 4x4 multiplied by the number 100, which denotes totality. The blood of Jesus was shed for all of creation throughout eons of time.

We have looked at the historical elements in 14:14-20, namely, Jesus the Son of Man and His crucifixion for all of creation which took place outside the city of Jerusalem. In the same passage John saw in his vision the spiritual dynamic of communion involving the interaction of Jesus and angels.

This interaction which John saw in his vision laid the groundwork for an understanding of the liturgical act of Holy Communion, which is much more than a *"memorial feast."* The Son of Man, wearing a golden crown, was seen sitting on a white cloud with a sickle in His hand. The triumphant Jesus (crown) is seen in His sinlessness (white cloud) with an instrument associated with the ingathering of Pentecost in his hand (sickle), (Deuteronomy 16:9-10).

Another called upon Him to reap the harvest of God's people. So the instrument of Pentecost's harvesting was the means used by Jesus to bring His people together. In Holy Communion God's people, His harvest, come together to celebrate their oneness in Jesus Christ.

Next, John saw another messenger (angel) from God's presence (Temple) with an instrument of judgment (sickle) in his hand.

(Note that in Joel 3:13 the sickle is also an instrument of judgment).

Another messenger (angel) of God came from the cross (altar) *"and called out in a loud voice to the angel with the sharp sickle, 'Thrust in your sharp sickle and harvest the clusters from the vineyard of the earth, for the grapes are fully ripe!'"*

The first reaping at the hand of the Son of Man was the gathering of those who are redeemed, while the second reaping at the hand of the angel was the expression of God's wrath in judgment, as described in the words, *"Then the angel swung his sickle upon the earth and gathered the harvest of the earth's vineyard, and threw it into the great winepress of the wrath of God,"* Revelation 14:19. God's wrath, which we sinners deserve, fell on the Son of Man, as verse 20 tells us.

In Holy Communion God's people, His harvest, not only come together to celebrate the victory of the spotless Son of Man who by the Holy Spirit has made us one, but also to give God thanks for Jesus, the sacrificial Lamb, on whom His wrath fell, *"so that in him we might,"* as Paul wrote, *"become the righteousness of God,"* II Corinthians 5:21.

The 144,000, God's elect, experience the reality of the words of the communion ritual as they "feed on Him in their hearts by faith with thanksgiving." This feeding on Jesus in Holy Communion is possible because the sickle in Joel's prophecy, which helps us interpret Revelation 14:14-20, was not only an instrument of judgment, but also an instrument of ingathering.

The harvest of ingathering which gave birth to the Church is evident in Acts 2:17-21, which describes the ingathering of God's people on the Day of Pentecost. The Holy Spirit in effect was God's sickle, as recognized by Peter, whose quotation in Acts 2:17-21 is taken from Joel 2:28-32. Because of the continuing presence of the Holy Spirit, God's people sing a *"new song"* whenever the Eucharist is celebrated. In doing so the Church recognizes that Jesus dwells with His people. The Lamb standing on Mt. Zion, 14:1, is an affirmation of the last words of the prophecy of Joel, *"The Lord dwells in Zion,"* Joel 3:21b. Thanks be to God!

Biblical Background for: Jesus, Avenger Of
God's Holiness
Revelation 15-16:11

Key Verse

*"Who should not reverence thee, O Lord, and glorify thy name? For
thou alone art holy; therefore all nations shall come and worship before
thee, for thy just judgments have been made plain!"* Revelation 15:4.

12 | Jesus, Avenger Of God's Holiness

Following the visions of chapter 14, which focus upon the central truth of the Christian faith, our Lord's sacrifice for sin, which is Jesus' gift to His Church celebrated in the *"new song"* of Holy Communion, verse 1 of chapter 15 speaks of *"another sign in Heaven"* described as *"vast and awe-inspiring"*. The signs of *Revelation* are of a superlative nature. 12:1 speaks of a *"huge sign,"* described in the NIV as *"great and wondrous"*.

It is the sign which *"became visible in the sky—the figure of a woman clothed with the sun, with the moon under her feet and a crown of twelve stars upon her head."* Soon after John beheld that sign, verse 3 of chapter 12 reads, *"Then another sign became visible in the sky, and I saw that it was a huge red dragon with seven heads and ten horns, with a diadem upon each of his heads."*

What was the purpose of the three *"vast and awe-inspiring"* signs which John saw, as recorded in chapters 12 and 15? The clue is found in what they reveal. They reveal that the power of a holy

God to overcome the forces of evil on behalf of His Church is awesome. The awesomeness of a holy God is evident in the signs of John's Gospel.

Concerning the first miraculous sign of changing water into wine John wrote, *"This, the first of his miraculous signs Jesus performed in Cana of Galilee. He thus revealed his glory, and his disciples put their faith in him,"* John 2:11.

Concerning the last sign recorded in John's Gospel, the raising of Lazarus, John 12:17-18, Jesus said to Martha, *"Did I not tell you that if you believed you would see the glory of God?"* John 11:40.

Previous to His conversation with Martha, Jesus had said to Mary and Martha before the raising of Lazarus, *"This sickness will not end in death. No, it is for God's glory so that God's Son may be glorified through it,"* John 11:4.

Finally, in John 20:30-31 it is written, *"Jesus did many other miraculous signs in the presence of his disciples, which are not recorded in this book. But these are written that you may believe that Jesus is the Christ, the Son of God, and that by believing you may have life in his name."* The purpose of the signs in *Revelation* is the same as those in John's Gospel.

The signs reveal God's glory and result in the glorification of God and of His Son. Where the Divine glory is there is no darkness. Evil is dispelled. Holiness prevails. Holiness prevailed when in the first *"huge sign"* of Revelation 12:1 the purity of the virgin mother Mary is emphasized in the description of her as being *"clothed with the sun."* Holiness prevailed when the huge dragon in chapter 12 was hurled down upon the earth, leading to the victorious cry in Revelation 12:10, *"Now the salvation of the power and kingdom of our God, and the authority of His Christ, have come!"* Holiness prevailed when the *"vast and awe-inspiring"* sign of Revelation 15:1 announced the final wrath of God against evil, when the chalices of God's wrath will be poured out upon the earth.

When John saw the seven angels holding the seven last plagues he also saw *"what appeared to be a sea of glass shot through with fire, and upon this glassy sea were standing those who had emerged victorious from the fight with the animal, its statue, and the number which denotes its name,"* Revelation 15:2.

John's vision of the fire and glassy sea, symbolic of holiness, and of believers who were victorious over the powers of evil, points to the honor that is due a holy God. Standing on the glassy sea those who *"emerged victorious"* are heard by John glorifying God as they sang the song of Moses and the song of the Lamb: *"Great and wonderful are thy works, O Lord God, the Almighty! Just and true are thy ways, thou king of the nations! Who should not reverence thee, O Lord, and glorify thy name? For thou alone art holy; therefore all nations shall come and worship before thee, for thy judgments have been made plain!"* Revelation 15:3-4.

Jesus vindicated the holiness of God, highlighted in the three signs, by receiving on the cross God's wrath, 14:19-20. This wrath we should have experienced because of our sins, Isaiah 53:5. Because of that deliverance, we sing a new song every time we receive the chalice of Holy Communion.

We are also shown through John's visions in Revelation 15 and 16 that God's holiness will be avenged when the chalices of His wrath are poured out on the unrepentant wicked.

The anticipation of the final elimination of evil is celebrated by God's victorious children, who sing the song of Moses and the Lamb accompanied by the harps given them by God. When, as one with those who have gone on before, we receive the cup of Holy Communion, we celebrate God's holiness as we proclaim the Lord's death until He comes again to judge the living and the dead. Every time we receive communion we celebrate what Jesus has done and will do to avenge and vindicate the holiness of God. The provision of eternal salvation by a holy God is the essence of the Church's proclamation.

The *"seven last plagues"* in the visions of John in chapter 16 are a capitulation of God's actions in history, which will eventuate in the final eradication of evil and the triumph of His Beloved City, the New Jerusalem. John explained that the outpouring of Divine wrath must be completed before anyone could enter the presence of the holy God, whose ways are *"just and true"*: *"The Temple was filled with smoke from the glory and power of God, and no one could enter the Temple until the seven plagues of the seven angels were past and over,"* Revelation 15:8.

Note in 15:8 the use of the number seven. It is the most significant symbolic number in the Bible. Its frequency in *Revelation* is evident to the most casual reader. In the *Apocalypse* there are over fifty sevens. Its importance is ingrained in creation itself, since the week has seven days, and the seventh day God blessed and made holy, Genesis 2:3. Furthermore, the holiness often associated with the number seven is emphasized by God's commands related to cleansing activity, as illustrated by Aaron's activity in connection with the altar of burnt offering, as recorded in Leviticus 16:19: *"He shall sprinkle some of the blood on it with his finger seven times to cleanse it and to consecrate it from the uncleanness of the Israelites."*

The number seven is also used in connection with God's judgment as illustrated by His promised sevenfold vengeance upon the slayer of Cain, Genesis 4:15. Because God is holy, salvation is not complete apart from cleansing and judgment. Jesus became the avenger of God's holiness when God's judgment due us was poured out on Him on the cross. Thus He satisfied the demands of God's holiness, making our cleansing from sin possible.

Since Jesus is the avenger of God's holiness, it was important for the Seven Churches of Asia and for the Church today to eat the bread and drink the cup of the Lord only after self examination. Paul wrote, *"For anyone who eats and drinks without recognizing the body of the Lord eats and drinks judgment on himself,"* I Corinthians 11:29.

It was, and is, essential that Christians through the power of the Holy Spirit walk worthy of the Lord, so that their eucharistic celebrations may help prepare them for the days of spiritual testing vividly described in Revelation 16.

It is the will of God that His holiness be seen in His children. I Thessalonians 4:3 reads, *"It is God's will that you should be holy."* Later in the same epistle Paul tells us the end God has in view when He sanctifies His people: *"May God himself, the God of peace, sanctify you through and through. May your whole spirit, soul and body be kept blameless at the coming of our Lord Jesus Christ. The one who calls you is faithful and he will do it,"* I Thessalonians 5:23-24.

According to Hebrews 2:10,18, Jesus, the author of our salvation, was made perfect through suffering; therefore, He is able to help His own in their trials. Can it be that the wrath of God described in Revelation 16, while directed against evil Babylon, is also intended to contribute to holiness of His children? I believe the context indicates just that.

John, in commenting concerning his vision of the seven angels holding the seven chalices filled with the wrath of God, says, *"The Temple was filled with smoke from the glory and power of God, and no one could enter the Temple until the seven plagues of the seven angels were past and over,"* Revelation 15:8. Before His children can enter the presence of a holy God, they must endure the trials that accompany the pouring out of His wrath upon the wicked. *"But he who stands firm to the end will be saved,"* Mark 13:13b. Furthermore, it is in the context of the outpouring of God's wrath that we read the words of Jesus, *"See, I am coming like a thief! Happy is the man who stays awake and keeps his clothes at his side, so that he will not have to walk naked and men see his shame,"* Revelation 16:15. Jesus, the avenger of God's holiness, is saying that Christians, passing through times of tribulation which precede His coming, must be vigilant in keeping the clothes of their righteousness unspotted by sin, lest others see their shame. The key imperative for God's children is *"Watch"*, (Mark 13:37).

Let us now consider the significance of the outpouring of the chalices of God's wrath for the Church of John's day, which serves as a warning for the Church today as well.

John reported that in his vision, when the first angel poured out God's wrath from the chalice, *"loathsome and malignant ulcers attacked all those who bore the mark of the animal and worshipped its statue,"* Revelation 16:2. From this first outpouring of wrath we learn that the plagues of Revelation 16 were directed against those who were identified with Satan and his allies. When we examine the forces of evil at work in the Church in the seven cities in the Province of Asia, something becomes apparent. Through John's visions the warnings and the offer of help from Jesus, the Lord of the Church, are given in light of our Lord's concern that the elect be aware of the importance of their faithfulness. They are to rely upon the strength of the Lord, lest they become apostate and fail to receive the blessings of God's eternal Kingdom—a heritage that has been promised to those who are overcomers.

That heritage was announced by Jesus, *"the holy one and the true"* through the angel of the Church in Philadelphia: *"As for the victorious, I will make him a pillar in the Temple of my God, and he will never leave it. I will write upon him the name of my God, and the name of the city of my God, the new Jerusalem which comes down out of heaven from my God. And I will write upon him my own new name. Let the listener hear what the Spirit says to the Churches,"* Revelation 3:12-13.

To the Church at Philadelphia and to all Christians who trust in and who are obedient to Jesus the promise is: *"I will keep you safe from the hour of trial which is to come upon the whole world to test all who live upon the earth,"* Revelation 3:10. The word *"from"* here does not suggest that the Church will not experience tribulation; but rather, it will be kept in the time of tribulation. In this sense it will be delivered from trials. This is in keeping with Jesus' petition recorded in John 17:15. Following this promise Jesus said to the Church of Philadelphia, *"I am coming soon; hold fast to what you have—let no one deprive you of your crown,"* Revelation 3:11.

From our Lord's words to the Church at Philadelphia, it is clear that the Church will be given strength by her Lord to remain faithful despite the onslaughts of the evil one. Furthermore, Jesus, the avenger of God's holiness, has made it possible for God's people to be holy, even as the Church experiences the shock waves of the outpouring of God's wrath upon the wicked—an outpouring as described in Revelation 16 which will *"test all who live upon the earth,"* Revelation 3:10.

God's holiness is avenged by His wrath which, in contrast to the chalice of blessing which believers receive in Holy Communion, I Corinthians 10:16, is the undiluted *"wine of God's passion"* (anger), 14:10. Christians are warned not to drink the *"cup of devils"*. I Corinthians 10:20-22 in the Phillips translation reads: *"I say emphatically that Gentile sacrifices are made to evil spiritual powers and not to God at all. I don't want you to have any fellowship with such powers. You cannot drink both the cup of the Lord and the cup of devils. You cannot be a guest at the Lord's table and at the table of devils. Are we trying to arouse the wrath of God? Have we forgotten how completely we are in his hands?"*

Lest the wrath of God also consume believers who, on the one hand, receive the chalice of Holy Communion and, on the other hand, dabble in paganism, Paul and John both warn the Church that it must be faithful, lest it also drink from the chalice of God's wrath.

Because the bowls referred to in Revelation 16 are libation bowls, I prefer to call them chalices. In that way the contrast between the chalice of blessing (Communion) and the chalice of wrath (judgment) is crystal clear. The writer of *Hebrews* wrote concerning the serious consequence to those who have begun the journey of faith, but who by their unfaithfulness have *"trampled the Son of God under foot."*

Hear the writer's strong warning in Hebrews 10:26-31: *"If we deliberately keep on sinning after we have received the knowledge of the truth, no sacrifice for sins is left, but only a fearful expectation of judgment and of raging fire that will consume the enemies of God. Anyone who rejected the law of Moses died without mercy on the testimony of two or three witnesses. How much more severely do you think a man deserves to be punished who has trampled the Son of God under foot, who has treated as an unholy thing the blood of the covenant that sanctified him, and who has insulted the Spirit of grace? For we know who said, 'It is mine to avenge; I will repay,' and again, 'The Lord will judge his people.' It is a dreadful thing to fall into the hands of the living God."*

John, as Revelation 16 indicates, was shown the nature of the judgments of the end times. There is a striking correspondence between the chalice judgments of chapter 16 and the trumpet judgments found in chapters 8 and 9.

The noteworthy difference in the first four judgments is that the chalice judgment destruction is total, whereas the trumpet judgments devastate a third of the natural environment. The message clearly indicates that the judgments associated with the fall of Rome would be less severe than the judgments leading up to the final destruction of the kingdom of evil.

After the first four chalice visions are seen by John, he is shown judgments that will truly mark the beginning of the end of the kingdom of evil. The intransigence of the wicked even in the face of severe judgment is indicated by the words, *"...men gnawed their tongues in agony, cursed the God of Heaven for their pain and their ulcers, but refused to repent of what they had done,"* Revelation 16:10b-11. Beginning with the outpouring of the fifth chalice, for the first time God's judgment will be directed against demonic perpetrators of evil, as described by the words, *"Then the fifth angel emptied his bowl upon the throne of the animal. Its kingdom was plunged into darkness,"* Revelation 16:10a.

Now we are ready to observe through John's eyes, beginning with 16:12 and concluding with 20:10, how Jesus, the *"Faithful and True"*, Revelation 19:11, who is *"King Of Kings And Lord of Lords"*, Revelation 19:16, will destroy the kingdom of evil and in so doing will bring honor to God and the Lamb.

Biblical Background for: Jesus, The Mighty Conqueror
Revelation 16:12-21 and 17

Key Verse

"They will all go to war with the Lamb, and the Lamb, with his called, chosen, and faithful followers, will conquer them. For he is Lord of lords and King of kings," Revelation 17:14.

13 | Jesus, The Mighty Conqueror

"*Babylon the great,*" Revelation 16:19, is the epitome of evil that John knew must be confronted and destroyed by Jesus if the Kingdom of our Lord and His Christ is to prevail, making possible the salvation of God's people. The cross of Jesus was the place where Babylon's destruction was made certain.

Paul, in writing to the Colossians, expressed eloquently the doom of the evil which Babylon represents when he wrote, "*He forgave us all our sins, having canceled the written code, with its regulations, that was against us and that stood opposed to us; he took it away, nailing it to the cross. And having disarmed the powers and authorities, he made a public spectacle of them, triumphing over them by the cross,*" Colossians 2:13b-15.

As previously mentioned in connection with the name Babylon in chapter 14, the Babylon of John's day was Rome. With this interpretation most ancient and modern Biblical scholars agree, and for good reason.

Babylon was an ancient nemesis of God's people Israel, while Rome was the oppressor of the Church of John's day. The description of the power, influence and mercantile activity, and even the seven hills on which Babylon sits, 17:9, all point to Rome as the city given the code name Babylon. While the immediate reference is no doubt to Rome, other cities since the fall of Rome can be cited as centers of great evil influence. Indeed the motif of final judgment which follows Babylon's destruction would suggest that Babylon, described as *"Babylon The Great, Mother Of All Harlots And Of The Earth's Abominations,"* Revelation 17:5, is to be regarded as the embodiment of all centers of earthly power under the sway of Satan.

Using the Babylon motif as symbolic of all the forces of evil arrayed against the Church is given credence by the outpouring of the sixth chalice, described by the words, *"Then the sixth angel emptied his bowl upon the great river Euphrates. The waters of that river were dried up to prepare a road for the kings of the East. And then I noticed three foul spirits, looking like frogs, emerging from the mouths of the dragon, the animal, and the false prophet. They are diabolical spirits performing wonders, and they set out to muster all the kings of the world for battle on the great day of God, the Almighty. So they brought them together to the place called in Hebrew, Armageddon,"* Revelation 16:12-14,16.

It is evident in this vision that the stage is being set for the final onslaught of evil in all of its demonic forms, under the Old Testament rubric of Judah's downfall at the hands of the mighty Babylonian Empire under King Nebuchadnezzar. How fitting too that the vision should incorporate the imagery of Armageddon.

The word Armageddon means Hill of Megiddo. The site of ancient Megiddo, where archaeologists have identified 20 layers where cities existed that were destroyed by wars, overlooks the southwestern edge of the plain of Esdraelon, which is in the shape of a triangle 15 by 15 by 20 miles. In this area many battles have been fought, including a battle in Israel's War of Independence in 1948. In every respect it seems appropriate to be seen in John's vision as the site of the last great struggle between the powers of good and evil.

When the seventh and last of the chalices was emptied, it resulted in a cataclysm of universal proportions, in contrast to the devastation initiated by the blowing of the trumpets in chapters 8 and 9, which affected one–third of the natural environment and human life. This points to what has already been observed, namely, that chapters 8 and 9 focused on the fall of Rome, a city which under the judgment of God would cease to exist as a mighty empire; while chapter 16 in John's vision depicts the larger picture of evil's downfall, which is prophesied in greater detail in chapters 17-20.

The Divine countdown of the destruction of the forces of evil, anticipated in 14:8, now is given momentum in John's vision recorded in chapter 17. We learned concerning the doom of those who receive the mark of the animal in chapters 15 and 16. Next in chapters 17-19 we learn about the fate of the sea-born animal, false prophet and the *"mother of all harlots"*, Babylon, who was *"riding upon a scarlet animal, covered with blasphemous titles and having seven heads and ten horns,"* Revelation 17:3.

She was exquisitely dressed, elaborately adorned with jewels and drunk with the blood of the martyrs of Jesus. As a symbol of the world's luxury, vice and culture Babylon seduced and enticed. She was the embodiment of *"the cravings of sinful man, the lust of his eyes and the boasting of what he has and does,"* I John 2:16.

John, who was inspired by the Spirit on the Lord's day when the Son of Man told him to write down what he saw and send it to the Seven Churches, 1:10, was carried away by the same Spirit into the desert where he saw Babylon riding on the scarlet animal. He now found himself face to face with the worldly representation of all that is opposed to the Son of Man, Jesus. While the message of the impending destruction of Rome given in chapter 9 was a comfort to the Churches of Asia, the Church then and now needs to hear that one day when our Lord's redemptive work leading up to and following the Lamb's sacrifice is complete, the forces of evil will be destroyed and Jesus will return to claim His Bride the Church, God's New Jerusalem, His *"Beloved City,"* Revelation 20:9.

Though Babylon, I believe, represents all the political, cultural and commercial powers of earth that are under the control of the dragon in the last days, for the Church of John's day the main center of the hydra of evil was Rome, which was built on seven hills. The angel told John that the seven horns of the beast on which Babylon rode were seven hills.

Most interpreters identify the hills with Rome's location. The angel also said that the horns represent *"seven kings; five have been dethroned, one reigns, and the other has not yet appeared—when he comes he must remain only for a short time. As for the animal which once lived but lives no longer, it is an eighth king which belongs to the seven, but it goes to utter destruction,"* Revelation 17:9-11. There are many interpretations as to who or what the numbers seven, five, and eight refer to in this passage. I believe they refer to the following Roman emperors: Caligula, 37-41 A.D.; Claudius, 41-54; Nero, 54-68; Vespasian, 69-79; Titus, 79-81; Domitian, 81-96; Decius, 249-251; and Diocletian, 284-305.

These eight emperors ("kings") are the ones most responsible for initiating and carrying out policies related to the relentless persecution of the Church prior to the conversion of the Roman emperor, Constantine.

I begin with Caligula, because during the reign of his predecessor, Tiberius, little attention was paid to Christianity by the Roman government. Jews enjoyed the free exercise of their religion, and Judaism and Christianity were indistinguishable to the average Roman.

Tiberius' predecessor, Augustus, did not consider himself to be a divine ruler and was insulted by the title *"Lord"*. Likewise, Tiberius did not permit anyone to address him as *"Lord"*. However, beginning in A.D. 40 Emperor Caius Caligula began to welcome the worship of his subjects. Later a statue of Zeus with Caligula's features was placed in the Temple in Jerusalem. The final step of self-deification occurred when he demanded that he be worshipped in Rome.

Writers referred to Caligula's successor, Claudius, as "our god Caesar." Nero, Vespasian and Titus also continued the encouragement of emperor worship as a part of a political cult. By John's time these five were dethroned. The state cult they had promoted was an unremitting threat to the Church. Open and very serious persecution was the order of the day under Caligula and Nero.

The reigning "king" in John's day was, of course, Domitian, who was the first emperor to demand that he be saluted throughout the empire as "Dominus et Deus", "Lord and God". He was the first emperor to demand directly that he be worshipped as a god. He was hailed as Jupiter's son and heir. Though it is not known that he engaged in any wholesale persecution of Christians, he did create a social and religious atmosphere inimical to Christianity.

Because the Christians could not condone as morally acceptable many of the practices commonly enjoyed by Roman citizens, they were suspected of being seditious, especially as they engaged in rituals that were often misunderstood. Because they were regarded as potentially dangerous to the state, the Church leaders during Domitian's reign were sometimes interrogated, arrested and even executed, or, as in John's case, banished.

Following the rule of Domitian, the operant behavior of succeeding Roman emperors was shaped by the pattern apparent in the political atmosphere created by Domitian, which saw the profession of Christianity as a possible capital offense. While these emperors did not initiate a general persecution of Christians, believers were sometimes executed for obscure reasons related to the belief that rejection of Roman gods would threaten peace and prosperity, and that the refusal to worship the emperor should be regarded as an act of treason.

During the third century, from 200-300 A.D., a quasi tolerance resulted in two periods of about 50 years each, when the Church enjoyed almost complete peace. However, during that time the Church also experienced two periods of the most severe persecution it had known.

Emperor Decius, 249-251, ordered the persecution of Christians and made emperor-worship compulsory. Emperor Diocletian, 284-305, ordered a general persecution of Christians. It would seem then that the words *"and the other has not yet appeared—when he comes he must remain only for a short time,"* Revelation 17:10b, is a prophecy pertaining to Emperor Decius. In A.D. 250 he was responsible for instigating the most violent persecution the Church had experienced up to that time.

However, this testing was short-lived, because within two years of the beginning of his reign Decius died in battle against the Gothic invaders from the north. But before his death Decius had required that everyone in the empire should get a certificate from an official indicating that he had sacrificed to the emperor. Death resulted in a refusal to obtain such a certificate. Thus Decius, more than any emperor before him, became the embodiment of antichrist.

Who is the "king" described by the prophetic words: *"As for the animal which once lived but lives no longer, it is an eighth king which belongs to the seven, but it goes to utter destruction?"* Revelation 17:11. The most likely candidate is Diocletian. He revived the cruelty of Nero and was the embodiment of the spirit of antichrist, who was doomed for destruction.

Rome's ending as a force to persecute Christians occurred when Emperor Constantine issued the Edict of Toleration at Milan in 313 A.D., which gave Christianity official status in the Roman Empire. Thus, Rome, the Babylon of John's day, ceased to trouble the Church.

John's concern for the Church was that it be faithful even in the midst of tribulation. The testing during Diocletian's reign was especially severe. Decrees of 303 pertained to church property, Christian books, Christians in the government and the army, as well as the clergy.

Another decree issued by the emperor in 304 ordered all Christians to offer sacrifices to the pagan gods. Christians in such far flung places as Palestine, Syria, Egypt and Asia Minor were martyred.

The price that believers had to pay for their faithfulness is illustrated by a man who was taking part in a play given before Diocletian in mockery of Christians.

When laughter broke out, he remembered what his Christian parents had taught him as a boy and shouted, *"I want to receive the grace of Christ. I want to be born again."* The people laughed louder, but the actor turned to the emperor and said, *"Illustrious Emperor and all you people who have laughed loudly, believe me, Christ is Lord."*

When Diocletian realized he meant it, he caused him to be tortured. Even as his sides were torn and burned with torches he kept on saying, *"There is no king but Christ, whom I have seen and worship. For him I will die a thousand times. I am sorry for my sin and for becoming so late a soldier of the true king."*

What do the ten horns represent in verse 12 where we read, *"The ten horns which you saw are ten kings who have not yet received their power to reign, but they will receive authority to be kings for one hour in company with the animal"?* Perhaps the reference is to the ten imperial provinces associated with the Roman Empire, as I previously indicated in the discussion of the animal from the sea in chapter 13. Though once they were totally subject to the power of Rome, during the last years of the empire both internal and external pressures caused the empire to unravel.

Rebellion became rampant as seething resentment was released; so former subjects began to feel they could shake themselves free from Roman domination, and indeed did play a role in Rome's fall. But even so, they ally themselves with Rome and the animal for a brief time *("one hour")* in a common goal to combat the Lamb. Their doom was assured.

Jesus, The Mighty Conqueror, enabled His Church to overcome, even as reported in Revelation 12:11, *"Now they have conquered him through the blood of the Lamb, and through the Word to which they bore witness."* In Revelation 17:14 the angel prophesies, *"They will all go to war with the Lamb, and the Lamb, with his called, chosen, and faithful followers, will conquer them. For he is Lord of lords and King of kings."*

Evil has within itself the seeds of destruction, and God's sovereignty over evil is absolute, are truths that are described with great power and clarity in Revelation 17:16-17: *"The ten horns and the animal which you saw will loathe the harlot, and leave her deserted and naked. Moreover, they will devour her flesh, and then consume her with fire! For God has put it into their hearts to carry out his purpose by making them of one mind, and by handing over their authority to the animal, until the words of God have been fulfilled."* John learned that the same seeds of self-destruction present in Rome would eventuate in the fall of Babylon.

Jesus, The Mighty Conqueror, was saying to the Church of John's day and ours what Jahaziel, through the Spirit of the Lord, said to King Jehoshaphat, *"Do not be afraid or discouraged...For the battle is not yours, but God's,"* II Chronicles 20:15. No wonder the animal, which is the embodiment of evil regardless of the form it takes, is seen in 17:8 as a pathetic parody of power headed for destruction. All those in league with the animal are doomed to fail whenever they engage in war against the Lamb, 17:14; for He is Jesus, The Mighty Conqueror!

Biblical Background for: Jesus, Honored By
Heaven And Earth
Revelation 18-19:10

Key Verses

"Then out of the throne came a voice, saying, 'Praise our God, all you who serve him, all you who reverence him, both small and great!' And then I heard a sound like the voices of a vast crowd, the roar of a great waterfall and the rolling of heavy thunder, and they were saying: 'Alleluia! For the Lord our God, the Almighty, has come into his kingdom! Let us rejoice, let us be glad with all our hearts,'" Revelation 19:5-7a.

14 | Jesus, Honored By Heaven And Earth

The dominion of the one called *"Faithful And True,"* Revelation 19:11, which gains for Him honor, is the emphasis of Revelation 9-20:10. Up to that point the focus has been on the glory of the Lamb which inspires worship.

Jesus has been seen as the One standing with His suffering people, enabling them to survive and remain steadfast, despite all the stratagems of the powers of evil.

The worshipping community in heaven and on earth offer Him glory and praise, as again and again the worthy Lamb enables God's children to be overcomers.

Now in Revelation 9-20:10, Jesus is seen as the One who, by His dominion over evil, receives in heaven and earth the honor that is His due, because of the utter defeat of Babylon and all the forces of evil.

Instead of a defender, Jesus is now seen as an active warrior who has *"come into his Kingdom,"* Revelation 19:6. Not only has He accomplished what needs to be done before the wedding day of the Lamb, but *"his bride (the Church) has made herself ready. She may be seen dressed in linen, gleaming and spotless—for such linen is the righteous living of the saints!"* Revelation 19:7-8.

Jesus' honor is seen in contrast to the fallen condition of Babylon. That honor will be upheld if the Church obeys the voice from heaven, which admonishes her in 18:4 to *"Come out from her, O my people, lest you become accomplices in her sins, and must share in her punishment."*

Babylon's rapid demise and total destruction is highlighted by the words, *"So in a single day her punishments shall strike her - death, sorrow, and famine, and she shall be burned in fire. For mighty is the Lord God who judges her!"* Revelation 18:8.

The first three verses of chapter 18 focus on the magnitude of Babylon's evil influence and the degradation of those nations in the end time who care only for the enhancement of their luxury and the experience of wanton pleasures. In their greed and lust they have *"become a haunt of devils, a prison for every unclean spirit,"* Revelation 18:2. No longer will they be enriched through commercial activity which included *"the very souls of men,"* Revelation 18:13.

The dirge of nations, that under the rubric of Babylon engage in excessive tyranny and self-love at the expense of God's people, is reminiscent of previous Old Testament prophecies concerning Babylon found in Isaiah in chapters 13, 21, 47. In reading this dirge it is well to contrast the condition of Babylon with the appearance of the angel who *"cried in a mighty voice: 'Fallen, fallen is Babylon the great!'"* John said concerning his vision of the angel, *"Later I saw another angel coming down from Heaven, armed with great authority. The earth shone with the splendor of his presence,"* Revelation 18:1. What a setting this section of *Revelation* is which accentuates the honor of the one who John said is called *"Faithful And True"!*

The honor of Jesus, the Faithful And True, is highlighted by the words, *"Pay her back in her own coin—yes, pay her back double for all that she has done! In the cup which she mixed for others mix her a drink of double strength! For the pride in which she flaunted herself give her torture and misery!"* Revelation 18:6-7.

In John's vision Jesus more than repaid the allies of antichrist for all the misery they caused the Church. In verse 8 of chapter 18, it is clear that the fire referred to in 17:16, by which the animal and the ten horns will destroy Babylon, is due to the sovereign power of God who is the defender of Jesus' honor; for verse 8 reads, *"She will be burned in the fire. For mighty is the Lord God who judges her!"*

The honor of Jesus, the Faithful And True, is also highlighted in Revelation 18:9-10: *"Then the kings of the earth, who debauched and indulged themselves with her, will wail and lament over her. Standing at a safe distance through very fear of her torment, they will watch the smoke of her burning and cry, 'Alas, alas for the great city, Babylon the mighty city, that your judgment should come in a single hour.'"*

In Luke's description of the waning moments before Jesus' death on the cross he includes a picture of the response of observers in the words, *"When all the people who had gathered to witness this sight saw what took place, they beat their breasts and went away. But all those who knew him, including the women who had followed him from Galilee, stood at a distance, watching these things,"* Luke 23:48-49.

Those moments of lament, which wrenched the hearts of Jesus' followers who observed the suffering of Jesus on the cross, contrasted with both the terror and the overwhelming sense of doom of the uncommitted observers at the cross, and with the accomplices of Babylon who observed her destruction. While the followers of Jesus, mourned and no doubt were stunned by what they saw and heard, there appeared to be no terror on their part. Indeed, they sensed the innocence and righteousness of Jesus, as expressed by the centurion, who confessed, *"Surely this was a righteous man."*

The righteousness of Jesus evident to those who saw Him die on the cross, and the glory of the kingdom of God, were vindicated by what John saw in his vision concerning the ending of the ignominious empire of evil. Babylon's destruction highlighted the honor due Jesus, the Faithful And True.

Babylon's vaunted power and proud luxury ended quickly, described in John's vision as destruction that occurred in a *"single hour"*. The lamentation, reminiscent of Ezekiel's doom song in Ezekiel 26, 27, is the cry of kings of earth in verses 9-10; merchants of earth in verses 11-17; and ship owners and sailors in verses 17-19. A brutal empire of evil could no longer indulge its clients' tastes with the opulence of exotic wares at the expense of the labors of slaves. Is it not the voice of Jesus which John heard say, *"Rejoice over her fate, O Heaven, and all you saints, apostles and prophets! For God has pronounced his judgment for you against her!"* Revelation 18:20?

As the description of the fall of the great city of Babylon concludes there is a striking parallel between Revelation 18:21 and Jeremiah 51:63-64. Verse 21 of *Revelation* reads: *"Then a mighty angel lifted up a stone like a huge millstone and hurled it into the sea, saying: 'So shall Babylon the great city be sent hurtling down to disappear for ever!'"* The *Jeremiah* passage reads: *"When you finish reading this scroll, tie a stone to it and throw it into the Euphrates. Then say, 'So will Babylon sink to rise no more because of the disaster I will bring upon her. And her people will fall.'"*

The contrast between the fate of the two Babylons is evident, too. The fall of ancient Babylon is described in terms of a defeat, whereas Babylon, which is a code name for Rome and all the humanistic forces of evil under the hegemony of evil, is dealt a final blow that results in her disappearing forever.

The victory of Jesus, the Faithful And True, is absolute and final. The victory over Babylon is so complete that everything in which a great city takes pride is brought to a grinding end. Never again will the arts and crafts bring joy. The illumination of light will be no more, and the voice of the bride and bridegroom will be silenced. Creative labor will end, and the luxuries of life made possible by commercial activity will cease. All this will occur, the mighty angel announced, *"For in her was discovered the blood of prophets and saints, indeed, the blood of all who were ever slaughtered upon the earth,"* Revelation 18:24.

All the "witchery" with which Babylon had seduced "all nations" would not save her. The echo of Isaiah's taunting words concerning ancient Babylon is heard by the Babylon of *Revelation*: *"Keep on, then, with your magic spells and with your many sorceries, which you have labored at since childhood. Perhaps you will succeed, perhaps you will cause terror,"* Isaiah 47:12.

Then Isaiah pronounced Babylon's doom in the words: *"Surely they are like stubble; the fire will burn them up. They cannot even save themselves from the power of the flame,"* Isaiah 47:14.

Concerning Babylon of *Revelation*, John recorded what he heard in his vision, *"Afterward I heard what sounded like the mighty roar of a vast crowd in Heaven crying: 'Alleluia! Salvation and glory and power belong to our God, for his judgments are true and just. He has judged the great harlot who corrupted the earth with her wickedness, and he has avenged upon her the blood of his servants!' Then they cried a second time, 'Alleluia! The smoke of her destruction ascends for timeless ages!'"* Revelation 19:1-3.

Babylon's fall was hailed in worshipful praise as a response to the *"vast crowd in Heaven"* by the Twenty–four Elders and the four living creatures who *"prostrated themselves and worshipped God,"* Revelation 19:4. Next a voice *"out of the throne"* called forth the praise of God from *"all you who serve him, all you who reverence him, both small and great!"* Revelation 19:5.

Heaven and earth in John's vision had joined in recognizing that *"salvation and glory and power belong to our God,"* Revelation 19:1. Why?, *"for his judgments are true and just. He has judged the great harlot who corrupted the earth with her wickedness, and he has avenged upon her the blood of his servants!"* Revelation 19:2.

The paeans climaxed, as described by John: *"And then I heard a sound like the voices of a vast crowd, the roar of a great waterfall and the rolling of heavy thunder, and they were saying: 'Alleluia! For the Lord our God, the Almighty, has come into his kingdom! Let us rejoice, let us be glad with all our hearts. Let us give him the glory, for the wedding day of the Lamb has come, and his bride has made herself ready. She may be seen dressed in linen, gleaming and spotless—for such linen is the righteous living of the saints!'"* Revelation 19:6-8.

John was so overwhelmed when the heavenly messenger spoke to him personally, *"Write this down: 'Happy are those who are invited to the wedding feast of the Lamb!'"* that he *"fell at his feet to worship him,"* Revelation 19:9-10. The heavenly creature who had spoken the words of God disowned the right to receive such honor as he said, *"No! I am your fellow servant and fellow servant with your brothers who are holding fast their witness to Jesus. Give your worship to God!"* Then he made it clear to John that he, like John himself, was only the witness of Jesus. In the process of being a witness of Jesus, Jesus Himself inspired his prophetic utterance.

Jesus is the Lamb who is worthy of the honor of heaven and earth. That worthiness earned for Him the title, *"Faithful And True"*. Therefore, though Jesus is not called by that title until 19:11, I have already referred to Him by that name in this chapter, which highlights His honored faithfulness, exhibited by the destruction of *"Babylon the great"*. Next, in a series of seven revelations that follow, John learned more about why Jesus, God's faithful and true Son, is worthy of the honor of all creation.

Biblical Background for: Jesus, Faithful and True
Revelation 19: 11-20:6

Key Verse

"Then I saw Heaven wide open, and before my eyes appeared a white horse, whose rider is called faithful and true, for his judgment and his warfare are just," Revelation 19:11.

15 | Jesus, Faithful And True

Beginning with 19:11 the *Revelation of Jesus Christ* focuses on the Church's head in seven wonderful ways. Each of these revelations begins with the introductory words *kai eidon*, Greek words meaning, *"and I saw."* The first three revelations show who Jesus is, 19:11, 17, 19. The next three revelations show what He does on behalf of His Church, 20:1, 4, 11. The last revelation, 21:1, points to the finality of Jesus. Presently, we shall look at the first five revelations that mark Him as the Faithful And True.

In the first revelation, Jesus, the Faithful And True, in 19:11 is seen in an open Heaven as the One who goes forth on a white horse to judge and make war. As the Church's Savior, Jesus repeatedly gives Himself through Holy Communion, which recalls for our remembrance that at the cross He was thrown *"into the great winepress of the wrath of God,"* Revelation 14:19. But now in 19:15 the process is reversed. He Himself is pictured treading *"the winepress of the furious wrath of God the Almighty."* The One who shed His blood on behalf of the Church by taking her punishment now is depicted in John's vision as the one who inflicts God's wrath on the wicked.

In 5:12 the whole company of heaven cries, *"Worthy is the Lamb who was slain, to receive power and riches and wisdom, and strength and honor and glory and blessing!"*

The description of Jesus in 19:11-16 indicates that truly He is endowed with power and strength, and indeed is worthy to receive those gifts and more. His power is symbolized by *"many diadems upon his head,"* Revelation 19:12. His spiritual strength is described by the prophetic word, *"He will shepherd them 'with a rod of iron,'"* Revelation 19:15. His sovereign greatness is celebrated by the description of Him in verse 16 as *"King Of Kings And Lord Of Lords"*.

In the second revelation of Jesus in 19:17 He is revealed as the Church's Lord. Verses 17 and 18 read: *"Then I saw an angel standing alone in the blazing light of the sun, and he shouted in a loud voice, calling to all the birds flying in mid air: 'Come, flock together to God's great feast! Here you may eat the flesh of kings and captains, the flesh of strong men, of horses and their riders—the flesh of all men, free men and slaves, small and great!'"* In contrast to the eucharistic feast of God's children which points to Jesus as Savior, the *"angel standing alone in the blazing light of the sun"* invited *the "birds flying in mid air"* to feast on the flesh of the enemies of Jesus. The invitation to the birds of prey reminds the reader of Ezekiel's words in Ezekiel 39:17-20. Those who resist Jesus' lordship will experience complete destruction. Those who do not honor Jesus as Lord will die in dishonor.

The third revelation of Jesus, beginning with 19:19 and continuing through to the end of the chapter, depicts Jesus as God's warrior. Jesus is seen in John's vision throwing antichrist and the false prophet *"into the lake of fire that burns with sulfur."* Furthermore, the evil cohorts of antichrist and the false prophet were killed with the sword of truth that came forth from the mouth of Jesus, the Word, 1:16, 19:15.

So through John's testimony we learn that Jesus, whose name is the Word of God, (Revelation 19:13), will one day counter the enemies of the Church by slaying the evil ones who oppose Him, and by throwing the chief henchmen of the dragon into the fiery lake of His wrath.

Through His self-revelation Jesus, the Faithful And True, revealed Himself as *"King Of Kings And Lord Of Lords,"* Revelation 19:16. Concerning Jesus, *"ruler of kings upon earth,"* Revelation 1:5, and *"someone like a Son of Man,"* Revelation 1:13, the prophet Daniel wrote: *"In my vision at night I looked, and there before me was one like a son of man, coming with the clouds of heaven. He approached the Ancient of Days and was led into his presence. He was given authority, glory and sovereign power; all peoples, nations and men of every language worshiped him. His dominion is an everlasting dominion that will not pass away, and his kingdom is one that will never be destroyed,"* Daniel 7:13-14. Jesus' absolute power and authority, which John and Daniel wrote about, is declared in words chiseled on the base of an obelisk which stands in the center of the square in front of St. Peter's in the Vatican. The words are:

Christus Vincit
Christus Regnat
Christus Imperat

The Latin means: Christ Conquers; Christ Rules; Christ Commands.

The fourth revelation of Jesus in 20:1-3 pertains to the binding and setting free of Satan. The fifth revelation in 20:4-6 announces the thousand year reign of Jesus with faithful martyrs of the Church. Revelation 20 is a fleshing out of what it means for Jesus, the Faithful And True, to be *"King Of Kings And Lord Of Lords"*.

Any interpretation that puts Jesus, King of Kings, on an earthly throne would be contrary to the spirit of not only *Revelation*, but also of the Gospels. *"Jesus said, 'My Kingdom is not of this world.'"* This declaration in John 18:36 is just as valid in *Revelation* as it was when Jesus stood before Pilate.

Jesus' rule is over a spiritual Kingdom, His Church. Those who hold fast to the witness of Jesus that centers in Him as the One sent from God belong to His Kingdom, 19:10. Jesus' testimony is true, for He was given the *"Spirit without limit"*. So John the Baptist pointed to Jesus as the One through whom eternal life is given when persons believe in Him, John 3:31-36. Jesus was not revealed to John the Seer of *Revelation* as fulfilling a new role on earth. Of Him John the Baptist testified, *"The one who comes from above is above all; the one who is from the earth belongs to the earth, and speaks as one from the earth. The one who comes from heaven is above all,"* John 3:31. No where in Scripture is it revealed that Jesus will reign on earth. He reigns in His people and over His people as head of the Church.

Not only is the Kingdom of Heaven characterized by His rule in and over His people, but also by the fact that He has dominion over the powers of evil. The resurrection of Jesus from the dead was a confirmation of that power, for through His resurrection He was declared to be the Son of God the Father, as prophesied in Psalm 2:7 and attested to by the Apostle Paul in Acts 13:33-34. In this position of power Jesus binds Satan, 20:2, and sets him free, 20:3, 7. Finally, in God's time Satan's doom will be complete, 20:10.

As with all of *Revelation*, the twentieth chapter has special meaning for the Church of John's day. When John was banished to the Isle of Patmos during the reign of Domitian, the future of the Church looked bleak. If he had been living in the fourth Century A.D., when Diocletian was Emperor of Rome, the prospects for Christianity would have been seen as even more dim. Trials, tortures, deaths, as well as continuous persecution magnified by restrictive laws, were the order of the day. Yet, on the horizon was the conversion of the Roman Emperor Constantine to the Christian faith. Soon thereafter the city Byzas, a word that gave Byzantium its name, would be renamed Constantinople after the first Roman Christian Emperor.

The city Constantinople stood at the center of a thousand years of Byzantine history. Whichever ruler sat on the imperial chair at St. Sophia, he was regarded as God's regent on earth. Even when he did not always agree with the Church, he was a Christian, and more than that, the head of the Eastern Church. Christianity was not only preserved during this millennium, but foes who were sometimes successful in their military confrontations with Byzantium, among them Serbs and Bulgarians, themselves became Christians. During this period, even when morality was at a low ebb, the Church never surrendered its basic principles nor its independence.

Does the thousand years of Byzantine dominance find its prophetic pattern in Revelation 20? One might think so, considering the fact that Byzantium encompassed the area where the Seven Churches of *Revelation* were located. The period of time, approximately eleven–hundred years, when the empire flourished, rounds out to thousand. Jesus indeed reigned during that period in the sense that His Church never ceased to be the dominate religious influence of the empire. Foes were either assimilated or defeated by Byzantium. Invading Asian peoples were kept out of most of the European continent. Law, codified by Emperor Justinian, gave the empire stability. Christian Byzantine scholars and artists were among those who injected new life into nearly every nation of the time.

Despite the case for the prophetic fulfillment of Revelation 20 made in the preceding paragraph, I am not willing to conclude that this interpretation is the only valid one. Even as such terminology as Babylon, tribulation, antichrist and false prophet may be regarded as multi-faceted, so it is with the term millennium.

Ten has often been regarded as a rounded figure for an amount greater than a few. Multiples of ten emphasize the "manyness" or magnitude of the issue at hand. Thus, the reign of Jesus for thousand years may be regarded in a manifold sense as including the fullness of God's Kingdom on earth. It would include the 144,000 representing the fullness of God's people, including representatives from all the tribes of Israel, reflecting the addition of many Jews to the Body of Christ, His Church, in the last days, Romans 11:26. Even from Ishmael's line there will be a remnant from Edom, Israel's implacable foe, that will come under David's tent, Amos 9:11-12. There will be those who ascend Mt. Zion to proclaim salvation to Edom (Esau), Obadiah, verse 21.

Paul wrote that God has exalted Jesus to the highest place *"that at the name of Jesus every knee should bow, in heaven and on earth and under the earth, and every tongue confess that Jesus Christ is Lord, to the glory of God the Father,"* Philippians 2:10-11.

This acknowledgment before the curtain of time falls will be the ultimate climax of the thousand year reign of Jesus. Logically, this general acknowledgment of the Lordship of Jesus by His foes, as well as His own, will occur after the final triumph of God's Kingdom, described in 20:7-10. Thus we see that 1000 is a concomitant term of fullness which includes both the full number of the elect drawn by God's Spirit, and the fullness of time during which the elect are drawn and the Lordship of Jesus is acknowledged by all.

The interpretation of *Revelation*, chapter 20 in particular, has suffered from two things: the desire to establish a sequence of events, and the need to pinpoint exactly where and how those events are to occur. So for example, appointed judges mentioned in 20:4 are seen by some interpreters sitting on thrones to judge as one would judge in a judicial court setting.

Must it be insisted that in such a setting either the apostles, Matthew 19:28, or unnamed saints, I Corinthians 6:2-3, are to be the judges? Or does John's vision simply suggest that the righteous are foils who are recognized for their deeds?

If it is known that apocalyptic literature within the Bible has an affinity with apocalyptic literature from other sources, then it may be obvious to the interpreter that a locus or a chronological order need not be established.

Neither does judging have to be understood in terms of a World War II Nuremburg trial format, designed to establish moral culpability. For example, the apocalyptic Qumran writers, representing a sect of Judaism, did not write as one composes a narrative. They viewed their Teacher of Righteousness, whose identity is still debated by scholars, as the purveyor of esoteric truth pertaining to the end times. The imagery of their writings was largely unintelligible to outsiders, especially if they sought to interpret everything literally. But for members of the Qumran community, theirs was a message of hope. So also it may be said concerning the revelations given to John by Jesus for His followers.

142

The outstanding New Testament scholar, Leon Morris, has pointed out that since the foreign over-lord would reject everything that was said, the apocalyptist sometimes even indulged in the wildest speculation. However, though John used images familiar to the apocalyptist like horns and crowns, he was inspired by the Spirit of God, Revelation 1:10, 4:2, 14:13, 17:3, 19:10, 21:10, 22:18-19. Morris understands this; so he points out that though *Revelation* has apocalyptic characteristics, nevertheless, John's visions convey the Word of God, 1:2, 19:9, albeit in a form that sometimes puzzles us.

John was inspired through the medium of his visions from Jesus to project truth already declared in the Scripture on the screen of the last days. So the victory of the Lamb, Jesus, is seen as providing the assurance of a final victory over the forces of evil, that are permitted under the sovereignty of God to lash out against the Church in diabolic fury that went far beyond the trials that John knew in his day. Even so, *Revelation* is basically optimistic, because it emphasizes the saving activity of our Faithful And True Lord Jesus that will result in the final salvation of His bride, the Church, 19:7-9. That saving activity even extends to lukewarm Laodecian types of churches, as He stands knocking at the door, (Revelation 3:20).

Verse 6 of chapter 20 speaks of the believer's first resurrection, the reference being to the new birth. Paul said we participate in Jesus' resurrection when we are baptized: that is, buried with Him in a death like His, in order that we may *"live a new life"*, Romans 6:4. This marks the beginning of the believers' reign with Christ. Once we die with Christ to sin and spiritually reign with Him, then the second death, *"the lake of fire"*, Revelation 20:14, *"cannot touch"* us, Revelation 20:6.

By reigning with Christ as victors over sin and death we give honor to Him. As members of His Church we participate in the fullness of God's Kingdom on earth, apocalyptically described as our thousand year reign with Christ. In this relationship with Jesus we are *"happy and holy"* as a result of our first resurrection, (Revelation 20:6).

Our joy and freedom from sin's condemnation we owe to Jesus, the One Faithful And True, who has redeemed us from the first death, spiritual death, which is present in all the offspring of Adam and Eve due to original sin, Psalm 51:5. As His redeemed ones we are privileged to be *"priests of God and of Christ"*, serving as representatives of His Kingdom on earth, Revelation 20:6, acknowledging Him to be *"King Of Kings And Lord Of Lords,"* Revelation 19:16.

This Jesus, who revealed Himself to John, cares for churches of our day which, like the Church of Laodicea, are diseased by the blight of spiritual lethargy. Jesus stands knocking at their doors, not only offering His loving presence, but also promising them the privilege of reigning with Him, the Faithful And True, if they will repent and shake off their complacency.

Biblical Background for: Jesus, Rescuer Of
His Beloved City
Revelation 20:7-10

Key Verse

*"They came up and spread over the breadth of the earth; they encircled
the army of the saints defending the beloved city. But fire came down
from the sky and consumed them,"* Revelation 20:9.

16 | Jesus, Rescuer Of His Beloved City

Before the New Jerusalem comes to earth, the forces of evil must be dealt a final blow. This phase of the demonstration of Jesus' dominion which completed the downfall of evil principalities and powers, earning for Him the supreme honor of Heaven and earth, is highlighted in verses 7-10 of chapter 20. True, the antichrist (animal or beast from the sea, 13:1-8, 17:3, 19:19-20) and the false prophet (animal or beast from the earth, 13:11-17, 19:19-20) in John's vision *were thrown alive into the lake of fire which burns with sulfur"*; but now in John's vision the dragon, the devil or Satan, is *"set free for a little while,"* only to suffer the same fate as antichrist and the false prophet.

Even though the prophetic element is present in *Revelation*, we must remember that the *Apocalypse (Revelation)* does not contain prognostications about chronological events in history, as though the apocalyptic message were reportorial, rather than the proclamation it is. Therefore, we need not spend an inordinate amount of time looking for a mysterious person somewhere in the world called antichrist, who is yet to make his appearance. The epistles of John use the word antichrist to refer to that spirit in the world which is contrary to the spirit of Christ, I John 2:18, 22, 4:3, II John 7. In Jesus' discussion of the end times He spoke of false Christs and false prophets. Note the plural. He said, *"False Christs and false prophets will appear and perform great signs and miracles to deceive even the elect—if that were possible,"* Matthew 24:24.

What is new in John's proclamation in the *Apocalypse?* In John's visions the activity of antichrist and the false prophet intensifies as the end draws nearer. The 666 (the humanist number) will be stamped more and more on the foreheads (minds) and hands (human activities of persons) of those who worship the idols of secularism, which are mentioned in II Timothy 3:1-7.

This is the message which Jesus gave John through the visions of *Revelation.* Though the proclamation by John relates to the question of Jesus, *"When the Son of Man comes, will he find faith on the earth?",* Luke 18:8, Jesus also says in Luke 18:7,8 that His chosen ones *"who cry out to him day and night"* will *"get justice, and that quickly."* This is the message of encouragement to the Church which John reiterates throughout *Revelation,* but especially here in Revelation 20:10, where it is proclaimed that the devil will suffer the same fate as the antichrist and false prophet.

Jesus will not only reveal the perfidy of the evil trinity so that they will deceive no more, but they will also be rendered totally inoperative. Their rejection by the Sovereign of the universe will be their eternal torment.

Again, note that mercifully for God's people, the last flash of demonic fury will be *"for a little while,"* Revelation 20:3. Jesus said, as recorded in Matthew 24:21-22, concerning the last onslaught of the evil one: *"For then there will be great distress, unequalled from the beginning of the world until now—and never to be equalled again. If those days had not been cut short, no one would survive, but for the sake of the elect those days will be shortened."*

I still have not answered the question if the Scripture indicates whether the single embodiment of the antichrist and false prophet of *Revelation* will be actual persons identifiable as such.

The implication of *Revelation* and the preponderance of evidence elsewhere in the New Testament would indicate that the answer is "yes."

What did I mean, then, when I previously wrote, "Therefore, we need not spend an inordinate amount of time looking for a mysterious person somewhere in the world called antichrist, who is yet to make his appearance"? II Thessalonians 2:3 reads, *"Don't let anyone deceive you in any way, for that day will not come until the rebellion occurs and the man of lawlessness is revealed, the man doomed to destruction."*

This would indicate to me that we are talking about an identifiable person, per se. But note that the one to be revealed as such, according to verse 6 of II Thessalonians 2, will *"be revealed at the proper time."*

We don't need to look for him, because he will be revealed. To whom? Persons of understanding, those of the elect who have insight that will prevent them from being deceived, will perceive who he is, Revelation 13:18. What we do need to be aware of is that *"the secret power of lawlessness is already at work,"* II Thessalonians 2:7. The lawlessness of which the antichrist is the quintessential embodiment is rampant everywhere throughout the earth right now.

The shocking reality is that very few of our political leaders would deserve a place in John Kennedy's *Profiles of Courage*. Self-aggrandizement is leading many of them to walk the path of vacillation and expediency. Ways are found to circumvent the law, and many blatantly spurn the law, if it is deemed necessary to do so in order to enhance their personal power. They often do so with impunity. When some are found guilty this does not deter other evil-doers who seek ways to avoid being detected. Few are willing to take personal responsibility for immorality, and many are only remorseful if caught.

The elect who have been called out of darkness into the marvelous light of Jesus need not be surprised if the antichrist, who will pass as a peacemaker, is honored as *"Time"* magazine's "Man of the Year".

What impedes the revelation of the antichrist? What or who is the restraining influence referred to in II Thessalonians 2:7? Paul in his letter to the Romans refers to common grace that is at work in the law, Romans 2:14-15. While the law can not save, it does accuse. It is this innate quality of life that is present in those whose consciences are not seared that acts as a restraining influence, and will continue to do so *"until the rebellion occurs and the man of lawlessness is revealed,"* II Thessalonians 2:3. In this way God for a time will restrain lawlessness *"until the rebellion occurs."* Neither is there any definitive indication who the false prophet will be.

John the Seer is not inspired by his visions to reveal unnecessary details. Only the role of the false prophet in relation to antichrist is described in *Revelation. Revelation* was not written to satisfy curiosity, or to provide answers for speculative questions. Each of the Seven Churches of Asia was told by Jesus what blessings would be given to the one who *"overcomes"*, or as in Phillips' translation, to the *"victorious"*. Calls to repentance, words of encouragement, and admonitions were all in the Seer's visions from Jesus, providing material primarily for John's proclamation to the Church of his day, but also to the Church of future generations.

The comforting, hope-filled, optimistic promise given to the Church at Smyrna was meant for the Church of every generation. Let the words reverberate which were *"spoken by the first and the last who died and came to life again"*: *"Be faithful in the face of death and I will give you the crown of life,"* Revelation 2:10. The opening words of Revelation: *"This is a Revelation from Jesus Christ, which God gave him so that he might show his servants what must very soon take place,"* Revelation 1:1, are followed by the first of seven beatitudes in *Revelation.* Verse 3 reads: *"Happy is the man who reads this prophecy and happy are those who hear it read and pay attention to its message; for the time is near."* The other six beatitudes are found in 14:13, 16:15, 19:9, 20:6, 22:7 and 22:14. John, the Seer and Scribe, saw himself as much in need of the *Revelation* of and from Jesus Christ as were his readers. He wrote, *"I, John, who am your brother and companion in the distress, the kingdom and the faithful endurance to which Jesus calls us, was on the island called Patmos because I had spoken God's message and borne witness to Jesus,"* Revelation 1:9.

What final event in the history of the struggle between good and evil would assure John and his readers that their faithful endurance was not in vain? The answer to that question is vital to all who desire to be obedient and faithful to Jesus, the Lord of Heaven and earth, and the head of the Church, His Beloved City. Revelation 20:7-10 is the answer provided by Jesus, who said, *"I hold in my hand the keys of death and the grave,"* Revelation 1:18.

The One who holds in His hand the keys of death and the grave says to us as He said to His captive people in Babylon, *"Listen...you who call yourselves citizens of the holy city...See, I have refined you, though not as silver; I have tested you in the furnace of affliction. For my own sake, for my own sake, I do this. How can I let myself be defamed? I will not yield my glory to another. ...I am he; I am the first and I am the last,"* Isaiah 48:1,2,10,11,12.

We are told in this key passage under consideration, Revelation 20:7-10, that at the end of history forces of evil, under the hegemony of Satan, and *"as numerous as the sands of the seashore,"* would encircle the *"beloved city."* The Beloved City is God's Kingdom on earth, His Church. Note that the forces of evil never enter that Kingdom, His Beloved City, to destroy it. Instead, God intervened and the forces of evil in John's vision were consumed by fire *"from the sky."*

How can we be certain that the Beloved City here is neither Jerusalem nor Rome? One clue is that Gog and Magog here are not localized. The theologian, G.C. Berkouwer, notes that in this prophecy Gog and Magog are not referred to, as in Ezekiel 38:2, as *"Gog, of the land of Magog."*

In *Revelation* the two names are merely associated with the four corners of earth from which Satan recruited his evil allies, through his skills of deception, to go to battle against the people of God. Another clue as to the identity of the Beloved City is the method employed to consume the evil foes of Jesus. The fire from the sky is referred to here as the method of destruction of the evil foes of God's Kingdom.

Paul, in writing to the Church at Thessalonica, commends them for their perseverance and faith in the face of persecutions and trials. He wrote to them that when Jesus returns they will be counted worthy, and that those who troubled them would themselves be paid back with trouble. He said, *"This will happen when the Lord Jesus is revealed from heaven in blazing fire with his powerful angels,"* II Thessalonians 1:7.

Paul's description of fire from heaven, at the time of Jesus' return, which is used to repay evil doers and to protect those who are worthy, corresponds to what is said in *Revelation* concerning the method God will use to protect His people.

Another striking parallel between these two passages, which serves as a third clue identifying the *"Beloved City"* as the Church, is that both passages are followed by descriptions of a final judgment. The Thessalonians passage reads: *"He will punish those who do not know God and do not obey the gospel of our Lord Jesus. They will be punished with everlasting destruction and shut out from the presence of the Lord and from the majesty of his power on the day he comes to be glorified in his holy people and to be marveled at among all those who have believed. This includes you, because you believed our testimony to you,"* II Thessalonians 1:8-10. So the parallel passage in II Thessalonians would suggest that God's people, His Church, comprise *"the Beloved City"* under attack by the devil and his allies prior to the return of Jesus in *"blazing fire"* to judge.

It would also appear that Peter, in II Peter 3, wrote about the same destruction by fire to which Paul and John refer. In his reference to the Day of the Lord Peter wrote, *"...the present heavens and earth are reserved for fire, being kept for the day of judgment and destruction of ungodly men,"* II Peter 3:7. Continuing this train of thought Peter used the same simile, *"thief,"* that Jesus used in 16:15, when he wrote, *"But the day of the Lord will come like a thief. The heavens will disappear with a roar; the elements will be destroyed by fire, and the earth and everything in it will be laid bare,"* II Peter 3:10. Our Lord's dominion over evil will then be complete. For that, all of creation will give Him honor.

Finally, Peter concludes chapter 3 of II Peter with moral exhortations in keeping with history's grand ending. By obeying Peter's exhortations the Church will truly be our Lord's Beloved City. He exhorts believers *"to live holy and godly lives as you look forward to the day of God and speed its coming,"* II Peter 3:11-12. He also admonishes believers *"to be found spotless, blameless and at peace with him,"* and warns them to *"be on your guard so that you may not be carried away by the error of lawless men and fall from your secure position,"* II Peter 3:14,17. Growth in *"the grace and knowledge of our Lord and Savior Jesus Christ,"* II Peter 3:18, Peter said, is in keeping with our "secure position." Obedience, Peter taught, is in keeping with the promise of *"a new heaven and earth, the home of righteousness,"* II Peter 3:13. Without our obedience, which Peter referred to in 3:2, Jesus' dominion over us is incomplete. Obedience is the hallmark of His Beloved City, the Church, because it is the only way that we can truly give Jesus the honor He is due.

SECTION III: POWER
Paradise For His Beloved City

Biblical Background for: Jesus, God's Appointed Judge
Revelation 20:11-15

Key Verse

"And then I saw a great white throne, and one seated upon it from whose presence both earth and sky fled and vanished," Revelation 20:11.

17 | Jesus, God's Appointed Judge

The truth of the completeness of Jesus' redemptive work is introduced by John's vision of the final judgment. All who have ever lived John saw standing before the *"great white throne"* to be judged. Who is the *"one seated upon it"?* Jesus answered the question, as recorded in John's Gospel, chapter 5 and verses 21-23: *"For just as the Father raises the dead and gives them life, even so the Son gives life to whom he is pleased to give it. Moreover, the Father judges no one, but has trusted all judgment to the Son, that all may honor the Son just as they honor the Father. He who does not honor the Son does not honor the Father, who sent him."*

This seminal passage in John's Gospel points to the final judgment by the Son as the last act of Jesus, whereby He will earn the honor of all persons who honor the Father. But now the focus is on the power of Jesus, for we are told, *"He who does not honor the Son does not honor the Father."* Furthermore, Jesus is seen as the one who *"gives life to whom he is pleased to give it."* This awesome power opens the door to Paradise for all believers. The Paradise lost in Genesis 3:22-24, now becomes Paradise restored, Revelation 2:7, 22:1-2.

Jesus Himself will call forth the dead and render final judgment: *"Do not be amazed at this, for a time is coming when all who are in their graves will hear his voice and come out—those who have done good will rise to live, and those who have done evil will rise to be condemned,"* John 5:28-29. Once that determination is made based on *"what was written in the books concerning what they had done"* Revelation 20:12, then all opposition to the Kingdom of our Lord will end; and by the power of Jesus Paradise will be fully realized.

The awesomeness of Jesus' power is emphasized by what John saw happen when His presence was revealed, as described by the words, *"from whose presence both earth and sky fled and vanished,"* Revelation 20:11. This revelation, John's sixth vision in this sequence, introduced by the words, *"And I saw,"* is followed by a description that depicts creation's power as being subservient to the Lord of Creation who initially called creation into being. The laws of nature fled at the moment of Jesus' resurrection. Again this is seen happening, as John witnessed, after Jesus the Judge returns. Concerning His return Paul prophesied in Acts 17:31: *"For he has set a day when he will judge the world with justice by the man he has appointed. He has given proof of this to all men by raising him from the dead."*

Jesus' awesome presence at the final judgment need not create fear in the hearts of those whose names are *"found written in the book of life."* John, in chapter 6 of his Gospel, records that Jesus three times in His Capernaum synagogue teaching spoke of the eternal bliss that would be God's gift to believers at the time of their resurrection. Hear the words of the Gospel: *"For my Father's will is that everyone who looks to the Son and believes in him shall have eternal life, and I will raise him up at the last day,"* John 6:40; *"No one can come to me unless the Father who sent me draws him, and I will raise him up at the last day,"* John 6:44; *"Whoever eats my flesh and drinks my blood has eternal life, and I will raise him up at the last day,"* John 6:54.

These same covenant themes of the Father's will, election, and the eucharistic presence of Jesus in communion we have already noted in *Revelation*. Together they are related to the power by which Paradise will be God's gift through Jesus, a gift which the Holy Spirit will impart to the Church, the bride of the Lamb, in the New Jerusalem.

The final expression of the awesomeness of Jesus' power related to the last judgment is described by the words, *"Then death and the grave were themselves hurled into the lake of fire, which is the second death. If anyone's name was not found written in the book of life he was thrown into the lake of fire,"* Revelation 20:14-15. The evil that is perishable is thrown into hell. This includes death and the grave, both of which are destroyed by the second death. That which separates the body from the spirit, death, will no longer be a blight on God's creation. That which imprisons the body, mortality, the grave, will no longer have power to do so, for as Phillips' translation reads in I Corinthians 15:51-57, *"Listen, and I will tell you a secret. We shall not all die, but suddenly, in the twinkling of an eye, every one of us will be changed as the trumpet sounds! The trumpet will sound and the dead shall be raised beyond the reach of corruption, and we who are still alive shall suddenly be utterly changed. For this perishable nature of ours must be wrapped in imperishability; these bodies which are mortal must be wrapped in immortality. So when the perishable is lost in the imperishable, the mortal lost in the immortal, this saying will come true: Death is swallowed up in victory. For where now, O death is your power to hurt us? Where now, O grave, is the victory you hoped to win? It is sin which gives death its power, and it is the Law which gives sin its strength. All thanks to God, then, who gives us the victory over these things through our Lord Jesus Christ!"*

The second death, hell fire, will be the fate of those whose names are not in the book of life, Revelation 20:15. Before being *"thrown into the lake of fire,"* spiritually speaking, their spirits were already dead. Jude, in verses 12-13, described their spiritual void in the words: *"They are clouds without rain, blown along by the wind; autumn trees, without fruit and uprooted—twice dead. They are wild waves of the sea, foaming up their shame; wandering stars, for whom blackest darkness has been reserved forever."* In effect they are nothing but flesh and blood. Paul said, *"I declare to you, brothers, that flesh and blood cannot inherit the kingdom of God, nor does the perishable inherit the imperishable,"* I Corinthians 15:50. Paul also said concerning the spiritually dead, *"They will be punished with everlasting destruction and shut out from the presence of the Lord and from the majesty of his power on the day he comes to be glorified in his holy people and to be marveled at among all those who have believed,"* II Thessalonians 1:9-10.

The power exercised by Jesus as God's appointed judge will secure Paradise for believers and prepare the way for Jesus as God's Omega to complete the Father's redemptive purpose for the Church by making all things new, as epitomized by the New Jerusalem. John saw the victory of the Church as being complete when God's servants, those redeemed by the Lamb and declared righteous by Jesus, *"shall reign as kings for timeless ages,"* Revelation 22:5. Through the power of Jesus this dominion is the final blessing of Paradise, His gift to His Beloved City.

Biblical Background for: Jesus, The Maker Of
All Things New
Revelation 21:1-21

Key Verses

"Then I heard a great voice from the throne crying: 'See! The home of God is with men, and He will live among them. They shall be his people, and God himself shall be with them, and will wipe away every tear from their eyes. Death shall be no more, and never again shall there be sorrow or crying or pain. For all those former things are past and gone.' Then he who is seated upon the throne said, 'See, I am making all things new!' And he added, 'Write this down, for my words are true and to be trusted,'" Revelation 21:3-5.

18 | Jesus, The Maker Of All Things New

We now come to that glorious part of *Revelation* that pictures all things new. John wrote, *"Then he who is seated on the throne said, 'See, I am making all things new,'"* Revelation 21:5. The old story of man's sin and struggle with the *"world, the flesh and the devil"* is over. In Revelation 21:1, the last and lengthiest of the seven revelations of Jesus beginning with the words, *"kai eidon"*, we see Jesus as God's finality. God's covenant blessings in Jesus are now fully realized, as John said, *"Then I heard a great voice from the throne crying: 'See! The home of God is with men, and he will live among them. They shall be his people, and God himself shall be with them,'"* Revelation 21:3. This important verse describes the intimacy of fellowship with God which characterizes newness. The writer of *Hebrews* realized that even before the perfect fulfillment of God's covenant promises, God's children on earth would experience a foretaste of covenant blessings. The promise of Hebrews 8:10 reads, *"This is the covenant I will make with the house of Israel after that time, declares the Lord. I will put my laws in their minds and write them on their hearts. I will be their God, and they will be my people."*

Paul, in writing to the Corinthians, stated the nature of the covenant heritage, which the Church knows in Jesus, clearly and positively in the following words: *"But as surely as God is faithful, our message to you is not 'Yes' and 'No'. For the Son of God, Jesus Christ, who was preached among you by me and Silas and Timothy, was not 'Yes' and 'No', but in him it has always been 'Yes'. For no matter how many promises God has made, they are 'Yes' in Christ. And so through him the 'Amen' is spoken by us to the glory of God. Now it is God who makes both us and you stand firm in Christ. He anointed us, set his seal of ownership on us, and put his Spirit in our hearts as a deposit, guaranteeing what is to come,"* II Corinthians 1:18-22.

The return to the pristine Paradise of Genesis 1 and 2 is described by the words, *"and the sea was no more,"* Revelation 21:1b. The sea for John was a symbol of conflict and strife among peoples and nations. It was the home of the animal in 13:1, and its waters were agitated by the harlot: *"As for the waters which you saw, on which the woman took her seat, they are peoples and vast crowds, nations and languages,"* Revelation 17:15. By the power of Jesus the peace promised to the shepherds: *"Glory to God in the highest, and on earth peace to men on whom his favor rests,"* Luke 2:14, was about to be realized; for John wrote, *"I saw the holy city, the new Jerusalem, descending from God out of Heaven,"* Revelation 21:2. At that moment yet to come, peace will forever prevail.

This New Jerusalem is indeed the Church, for it is the bride, the wife of the Lamb. Is not the New Jerusalem coming down from Heaven another example of God meeting man where he is? The God who conversed with Adam in the garden in the cool of the day is the same God who came into the world in the person of Jesus, who said, *"I have come to do your will, O God,"* Hebrews 10:7.

This New Jerusalem, made possible by the sojourn of the Lamb in Old Jerusalem, is everything the early Jerusalem was not. Old Jerusalem represented the pride of man. New Jerusalem shines as the glory of God. Old Jerusalem slew the prophets. New Jerusalem fulfills their prophecies. Old Jerusalem was a center of warfare. New Jerusalem is truly the *"city of peace"*. Old Jerusalem is temporal. New Jerusalem is eternal. Yet, were it not for the sacrifice of the Lamb carried out with the approval of the priestly authorities of Old Jerusalem, New Jerusalem would not have come into being. This was why Jesus left the bucolic ambiance of Galilee to enter Jerusalem, a city filled with seething hate and unsettling frustration. What the newspaper columnist Anna Quindlen said about the cities of our day could be said about earthly Jerusalem of Jesus' day and ours: *"Looking at our cities today is like looking into a deep abyss so deep that we get dizzy and recoil in fear and despair."*

The New Jerusalem in John's vision could be seen in its consummate splendor, because the first heaven and the first earth had disappeared. So the New Jerusalem, the Church, was seen *"descending from God out of Heaven, prepared as a bride dressed in beauty for her husband,"* Revelation 21:2. The bride's adornment was described in delightful detail in Revelation 19:7-8: *"...his bride has made herself ready. She may be seen dressed in linen, gleaming and spotless—for such linen is the righteous living of the saints!"* The Lord had granted to His Church an attire that was gleaming and spotless, symbolic of the righteous living of His people. With the fall of Babylon, and the hurling of Satan, the antichrist and the false prophet into the lake of fire, the wedding of Jesus and His bride the Church could be consummated, and the *"wedding feast of the Lamb"* could begin. Dying and mourning were no more. Instead of cries of pain and suffering, John heard: *"...a sound like the voices of a vast crowd, the roar of a great waterfall and the rolling of heavy thunder, and they were saying: 'Alleluia! For the Lord our God, the Almighty, has come into his kingdom! Let us rejoice, let us be glad in our hearts. Let us give him the glory, for the wedding day of the Lamb has come,...'"* Revelation 19:6-7.

Prior to that glorious day the Church of John's day and ours would have a foretaste of the wedding feast of the Lamb every time the Eucharist would be celebrated. In this sense the God revealed in Jesus is already *"making all things new!"* Therefore, in the light of what He was doing and would do, He admonished John to write down what he saw for the comfort of the persecuted Church. Then God added as He spoke from the throne, *"It is done! I am Alpha and Omega, the beginning and the end. I will give to the thirsty water without price from the fountain of life. The victorious shall inherit these things, and I will be God to him and he will be son to me,"* Revelation 21:6-7. *"It is done!"* is an echo of the word of Jesus from the cross, *"It is finished."*

Because of Jesus' atoning death on the cross, the fountain of His grace is open so that we may drink the water of eternal life, John 4:13-14. When God's people participate in the Eucharist they drink anew from the cleansing stream and *"proclaim the Lord's death until He comes,"* I Corinthians 11:26.

When He does come again the marriage feast of the Lamb will begin and last for all eternity. A blessed union between the Redeemer and the redeemed will result in a spiritual intimacy beyond anything we can imagine. Therefore, as we come to Communion and experience the joy of the New Jerusalem now, may the words of Hebrews 12:22-24 vibrate in our hearts: *"But you have come to Mount Zion, to the heavenly Jerusalem, the city of the living God. You have come to thousands upon thousands of angels in joyful assembly, to the church of the firstborn, whose names are written in heaven. You have come to God, the judge of all men, to the spirits of righteous men made perfect, to Jesus the mediator of a new covenant, and to the sprinkled blood that speaks a better word than the blood of Abel."* With this sense of coming to Mt. Zion through the sacrament of Holy Communion, Jesus will give Himself to us in such a way that we shall experience, as members of His Beloved City, a foretaste of the New Jerusalem.

We are now ready to walk on holy ground as we enter the New Jerusalem and catch with John a glimpse of Paradise. It is fitting that one of the angels who poured out God's wrath from a chalice now shows us, through John's vision, the splendors of the New Jerusalem. To John the angel said, *"Come, and I will show you the bride, the wife of the Lamb,"* Revelation 21:9. Then John described his journey in the spirit in the words: *"Then he carried me away in spirit to the top of a vast mountain, and pointed out to me the city, the holy Jerusalem, descending from God out of Heaven, radiant with the glory of God. Her brilliance sparkled like a very precious jewel with the clear light of crystal,"* Revelation 21:10-11.

The *"coming"* of the New Jerusalem is not the descent of a mysterious spiritual space station; rather, it is a symbolic description of the Church in all of its purified beauty occupying the lofty heights of perfect love made possible by its bridegroom Jesus, who has perfected His bride in accordance with the holy will of God. This life and beauty, which one day will mark the Church, was described in John's vision in the best way that human language and symbols will allow. Let's look now with John at its spiritual splendor and architecture. In so doing we shall worship and adore Jesus as God's Omega, who by the power of His love completes the work God gave Him to do. Before a description of the Beloved City, which has become the New Jerusalem, was given, Jesus spoke a word of warning regarding the exclusion of the works of darkness from the Holy City: *"But as for the cowards, the faithless and the corrupt, the murderers, the traffickers in sex and sorcery, the worshippers of idols and all liars—their inheritance is in the lake which burns with fire and sulfur, which is the second death,"* Revelation 21:8.

The New Jerusalem was described in terms of walls, gates and foundations. The walls and gates were not intended for safety, security or exclusion. Already we have heard a word concerning what will be excluded. The powers of evil were no more, and so there was no need for safety or security. These elements which were and are an important part of earthly Jerusalem are seen as a part of the splendor, beauty, harmony and orderliness of Heavenly Jerusalem. The number four has a vital part in the description, because it is the number of creation (four seasons; four points of the compass; four winds in Jeremiah 49:36, Ezekiel 37:9, Matthew 24:31; four corners of the earth in Isaiah 11:12, Ezekiel 7:2, Revelation 20:8). There are twelve foundations for the walls of the New Jerusalem, four x three, the four representing creation and the three representing our triune God. Each foundation was named after an Apostle. Taken together these numbers signify that God has created the New Jerusalem and has built its gates upon the foundation of the Word proclaimed by the Apostles. There are twelve gates, and over the gateways were inscribed the names of the sons of Jacob, the progenitors of Israel. What a vivid symbol of the importance of Israel in the redemptive plan of God, as has already been noted in comments upon the 144,000. We are reminded, too, that Jesus said, *"...salvation is from the Jews,"* John 4:22.

What is the significance of the measuring of the New Jerusalem? It provides a depiction of perfection which only Jesus, God's Alpha and Omega, can provide. Remember, the New Jerusalem is the Church, His Body. The work of Jesus on behalf of the Church is complete, perfect, final. John saw the angel measure the city with a *"golden rod"*. Gold denotes perfection. One can expect that the result of using a perfect measuring rod would be to show that the work of God's builder, Jesus, would reveal spiritual finality. Indeed the dimensions reveal completeness, perfection.

The New Jerusalem with twelve gates and twelve foundations has a wall which is 144 cubits high (12 x 12), or more than 200 feet, and its length, width and height is 12,000 stadia (1400 miles). Twelve expresses the unity between God and His new creation (three x four), the Church which will abide forever.

Note, too, that the perfection of the Church, and hence the finality of Jesus and His work is symbolized by the cube form of the New Jerusalem. Its height is the same as its length and width, and the city is made of pure shining gold, another symbol of perfection. The cube as a symbol of the perfection where God dwells, is illustrated by the Holy of Holies, the Temple's inner sanctuary, which under God's direction was built in the shape of a cube lined with gold, I Kings 6:20.

Consider the splendor of God's Beloved City which is now seen as the New Jerusalem: *"The street of the city was purest gold, gleaming like glass, 21:21b, and each gate was made of a single pearl. The wall itself was built of translucent stone,"* Revelation 21:18a. The twelve foundations on which the wall rested, and on which were engraved the names of the twelve Apostles were made up of twelve precious stones, 21:19-20. Likely all the stones John saw were translucent, and each gem added beauty to the whole. The first one mentioned, the iridescent jasper, has been called the gem of God because it draws to itself many shades of color which it reduces to unity. Does this not remind us that in this four–square city persons from all tribes and nations have come together in a beautiful blend of color, drawn to their beautiful Savior, Jesus, who is God's Omega?

Not only did the stones in the foundations add to the beauty of the New Jerusalem, but they also were intended to remind its inhabitants of the beauty of truth as it pertains to Jesus, God's final Word. For example, it is said that the sardonyx, an onyx with alternating brown and white bands of sard and other minerals, is the stone of fear. Man prostrates himself before God in shame in need of God's mercy; while the topaz is a symbol of the God of love we know in Jesus who forgives. God's final Word truly is in Jesus who forgives those who repent.

As in the stones on the Old Testament high priest's breast-plate, which are the same as the gems on the New Jerusalem's foundation, we see a heavenly power at work in the Church in the midst of a world in spiritual revolt against God and His Christ. The Church, is the beautiful bride of Jesus which is called to ho-liness in this life that it might serve as an instrument of God's judgment on a world that is under the influence of Satan. The stones on the bottom row of the high priest's breastplate were symbols of fear, humiliation and the need for repentance; while the stones in the rows above were reminders of what an encoun-ter of faith in God could do to bring about union with God, holi-ness and an understanding of truth.

God needs a faithful Church today to speak and live His Word of judgment and grace. This is foundational to the life of His Beloved City, the Church on earth. The Church must ever point persons to Jesus, God's finality, the Omega, who said, *"I am the way and the truth and the life. No one comes to the Father except through me,"* John 14:6.

In coming to Jesus, all things are made new as God's thirsty children drink of the water of life eternal.

Biblical Background for: Jesus, The Light And Life
Revelation 21:22-22:5

Key Verses

"The city has no need for the light of sun or moon, for the splendor of God fills it with light, and its radiance is the Lamb," Revelation 21:23.

"Then he showed me the river of the water of life, sparkling like crystal as it flowed from the throne of God and of the Lamb," Revelation 22:1.

19 | Jesus, The Light And Life

What does the future hold for the Church? Jesus, the Light And Life, is the Church's future. John said, concerning his vision of the New Jerusalem, *"I could see no Temple in the city, for the Lord, the Almighty God, and the Lamb are themselves its Temple,"* Revelation 21:22. The Church looks forward to the time when no sanctuary will be needed in which to worship God, because the sense of His majesty and glory in all of its fullness will be everywhere experienced through constant fellowship with God made possible by the Lamb. That constant fellowship will be evident in the appearance of those indwelt by Jesus, the Light And Life whose purifying presence makes persons fit to dwell in the New Jerusalem. Concerning those purified ones in the Church of Sardis John wrote, *"They shall walk with me in white, for they have deserved to do so. The victorious shall wear such white garments, and never will I erase his name from the book of life. Indeed I will speak his name openly in the presence of my Father and of his angels,"* Revelation 3:4b-5.

The *"splendor of God"* and the *"radiance"* of the Lamb fill the New Jerusalem with light, obviating the necessity of light from the sun and moon. Before that glorious day comes when the New Jerusalem radiates with Divine light, Jesus said to all who would follow Him, *"Put your trust in the light while you have it, so that you may become sons of light,"* John 12:36. Also Jesus said, *"I have come into the world as a light, so that no one who believes in me should stay in darkness,"* John 12:46.

Before the day comes when light will prevail, Jesus was saying that as children of light His followers need not *"stay in darkness"* even during those times of testing when the *"prince of this world"* seeks to destroy them. The Church's present is determined by its future which is ordained of God. Jesus had already said, *"...the prince of this world now stands condemned,"* John 16:11; and now He confirmed through John's vision that after the consequences of evil's condemnation are complete, the Church will dwell in the perpetual light of the Divine presence.

Furthermore, *"filthiness and lies"* will not mar that presence, for *"only those whose names are written in the Lamb's book of life"* will enter the city, Revelation 21:27. But the city of light will be open to nations and leaders of earth, so that they may walk in the city's light bearing as gifts the splendors, honors and treasures by which their glory has been defined. What a climatic testimony this will be to the glory, honor and power due the *"Almighty God and the Lamb."* Like the magi, they will offer the splendor of their gifts. As they honor God with the wealth with which God had already endowed them, the prophecy of Isaiah 60:11 will be fulfilled: *"Your gates will always stand open, they will never be shut day or night, so that men may bring you the wealth of nations—their kings led in triumphal procession."*

On this earth the Church experiences both periods of darkness and light, but even the light is not free of darkness. For John and the Church of his day Rome represented darkness. Centuries later, after the conversion of Emperor Constantine, a tolerant Rome brought light into the life of the Church. Even so, the darkness of evil was ever present. Many Christians compromised their faith and took on pagan ways. Rome itself became morally decadent, but the Church rejoiced that Rome was a buffer against the attacks of barbarian hosts. But the time came when a weakened Rome succumbed to the barbarians.

It was a summer evening, A.D. 410, in the Roman North African city of Hippo. Three men gathered for the evening meal in the monastery which stood by the great basilica where Christians regularly assembled to worship God. Aurelius Augustinus (St. Augustine), bishop of Hippo, was the host. His two guests were Alypius, his close friend and bishop of Tagaste, and Marcellinius, a Roman tribune and a sincere Christian. In the course of their time together the silence of nearby streets was broken by strident voices of persons who shouted staccato sentences. Out of the din came a messenger who crashed through the door of the refectory and shouted to Augustinus: *"Rome is fallen! Alaric and his Goths have sacked the Eternal City."*

After a brief period of silence, Marcellinius, the tribune, spoke, *"Rome is fallen. It is terrible, if not unexpected news. The barbarians will sweep over all the Empire. They will come across the Mediterranean. Nothing can stop them now. Hippo, too, will fall."* (In the year 430, Hippo was besieged by the Goths, and it too fell.)

Augustinus had not spoken. He seemed to be preoccupied with thoughts that took him beyond that traumatic moment. And then Alypius spoke, *"But if the mightiest of all earthly dominions passes away, what does remain?"* Augustinus answered, *"The City of God remains, and the Church of God through which that City is brought within this passing world."*

Augustinus continued his thought by contrasting cities that run their course in this life. He said, *"Two loves have built two cities; the earthly, which is built up by love of self to the contempt of God; and the heavenly, which is built up by the love of God to the contempt of self."*

Then as Augustinus spoke to his guests across the refectory table, he said, *"What we have heard today, my friends, is but one episode in this long story. There will be many more hours of judgment in the future history of the world, but in the end the City of God will stand. It is, it is now, and ever shall be! In the eternity of God is its life! In the truth of God is its light! In the goodness of God is its joy! In the unchanging love of God is its hope!"*

175

Augustine later developed these thoughts in his great theological treatise, *The City of God*. Much that he had to say no doubt was inspired by John's vision of the Beloved City, which became one with the New Jerusalem.

What or who is it that makes it possible for the city to experience the healing wholeness that God provides for His Church? God does this through Jesus, The Life. The same angel who had emptied one of the chalices of God's wrath but who later showed John the splendor of Jesus' bride, the Church, now, John said, *"showed me the river of life, sparkling like crystal as it flowed from the throne of God and of the Lamb,"* Revelation 22:1.

This pure water of life was the Holy Spirit who flows from God the Father and God the Son. The Spirit was given to the Church in accordance with the sovereign will of God (the flow of water was from the throne of God). The Spirit was given as a result of the redemptive sacrifice and resurrection of the Lamb (the flow of water was also from the throne of the victorious Lamb). At the Feast of Tabernacles Jesus said that His teaching was in accordance with God's sovereign will, John 7:14-18. After Jesus established His credibility, John wrote, *"On the last and greatest day of the Feast, Jesus stood and said in a loud voice, 'If a man is thirsty, let him come to me and drink. Whoever believes in me, as the Scripture has said, streams of living water will flow from within him.' By this he meant the Spirit, whom those who believed in him were later to receive. Up to that time the Spirit had not been given, since Jesus had not yet been glorified,"* John 7:37-39. The triune God, Father, Son and Holy Spirit, is the One who gives to the Church healing and wholeness.

If healing and wholeness are made possible through grace given by the Trinity, as symbolized by the stream flowing from the throne, what is the means whereby this grace is made available to sinful humankind lacking any merit and totally bereft of any reason to expect such grace? The answer is the cross on which the Lamb of God was sacrificed for the sins of the human race. The tree of life, *"in the middle of the street of the city and on either bank of the river,"* Revelation 22:2, represented the cross in John's vision. The same Greek word used for tree here in Revelation 22 is used for the cross in several New Testament passages, including I Peter 2:24, which reads: *"He himself bore our sins in his body on the tree, so that we might die to sins and live for righteousness; by his wounds you have been healed."* The Greek words translated tree of life literally mean *"wood of life"*. How efficacious this tree, His wooden cross, is! It bears fruit for the life and nourishment of God's children the year round. The nuance of the Greek would seem to suggest twelve kinds or varieties of fruit, as a number of translations indicate. If this is the case, the suggestion of the passage would be that the cross offers God's wholeness to persons afflicted with all kinds of bondage and spiritual disease.

What of the extent of the healing and wholeness which the cross provides? *"The leaves of the tree were for the healing of the nations,"* Revelation 22:2b. Whomsoever God touches through the stream of the Holy Spirit is given life by eating the fruit made possible by the tree, and is made whole by the healing leaves applied to the diseased parts of their personal lives.

Note that the tree symbolizing the cross was seen by John in the center of Paradise as an eternal reminder of the Church's source of spiritual life. Thus, Jesus' Beloved City will be characterized by wholeness and perfection. The New Jerusalem and His Beloved City will be one and the same. Before that great day, the Church's task on earth will be to proclaim the Lamb, sacrificed and victorious. This will be done through the proclamation of the Word and the celebration of the Eucharist. All those in the Church who are touched by God's healing grace have their names written in the Lamb's book of life.

The tree of life in Eden, which bore fruit that could not be eaten by the first Adam because of his disobedience, is now offered by the second Adam, Jesus, to fallen humanity through the merits of His obedience. Because of Jesus' obedience, Hebrews 10:5-7, what Ezekiel saw as the perfect, prolific fruit bearing ideal, Ezekiel 47:12, is now spiritually realized through the healing and wholeness which the Lamb, Jesus, made possible, I Peter 2:24. Because Jesus is God's Light And Life, John was able to declare with certainty, *"Nothing that has cursed mankind shall exist any longer. The throne of God and of the Lamb shall be within the city. His servants shall worship him; they shall see his face, and his name will be upon their foreheads. Night shall be no more, they have no more need for either lamplight or sunlight, for the Lord God will shed his light upon them and they shall reign as kings for timeless ages,"* Revelation 22:3-5.

There is no new thought or information in the paragraph contained in 22:3-5. But let the linkage be noted between the words of 22:5, *"...and they shall reign as kings for timeless ages"* and the words of 5:10b: *"and they shall reign as kings upon the earth."* The *"they"* in 5:10b has reference to "men from every tribe, and tongue, and people, and nation" who were purchased by the blood of the worthy Lamb who was slain.

The *"they"* of Revelation 22:5 has reference to God's servants who have been cleansed and sustained by the stream of water, the Holy Spirit, that flows from the throne of the Lamb. Thus we see that in this concluding section of *Revelation*, just before the epilogue which begins with 22:6, the focus is upon God's servants who belong to His Beloved City, the Church. One of the angels who had poured out God's wrath from a chalice, (Revelation 21:9), assured John that God's servants would worship Him through holy service and reign for endless ages, (Revelation 22:3,5). The groundwork for this felicitous outcome for God's Beloved City was laid previously when *"a loud voice came out of the Temple, from the throne saying, 'The end has come!'"* Revelation 16:17.

This announcement was followed by a description of the most catastrophic nature found anywhere in scripture in Revelation 16:18-21. This prelude to the final destruction of evil, as later described in Revelation 17-20, prepared the way for the time when it would be said of God's servants, *"... they shall see his face and his name will be upon their foreheads,"* Revelation 22:4. Thus Jesus, the Light And Life, will make possible the complete realization of John 1:4 (Phillips): *"In him appeared life and this life was the light of mankind."*

Biblical Background for: Jesus, The Morning Star,
The Church's Omega
Revelation 22:6-21

Key Verses

*"I am Alpha and Omega, the first and the last, the beginning and the
end,"* Revelation 22:13.

*"I, Jesus, have sent my angel to you with this testimony for the Churches. I
am both the root and stock of David, and the bright star of the morning!"*
Revelation 22:16.

Epilogue

Jesus,
The Morning Star,
The Church's Omega

The epilogue of Revelation is the setting for these words, which are a commission to the Church of every age: *"I, Jesus have sent my angel to you with this testimony for the Churches. I am both the root and stock of David, and the bright star of the morning!"* 22:16. The Greek word translated *"you"* is in the plural, indicating that all God's children have a responsibility to see that the testimony in *Revelation* given by Jesus through His angel is given to all the Churches.

Jesus, as *"the root and stock of David,"* came first of all to the House of Israel; but now His mission through us His children is universal, for He is also the *"bright star of the morning!"*

As such, like Venus, He is the *"light-bringer"* to all, rising before the dawn to herald a new day. To those in the darkness of sin's night who receive Him, He is the Morning Star who rises in their hearts to illumine them with God's truth, II Peter 1:19.

The *"testimony"* of *Revelation* which the Church needs to hear is built on the scaffold of Old Testament and New Testament history. An example of this would be the plagues of Egypt, which are a paradigm for the trumpets and chalices of *Revelation* which intensify and universalize the Old Testament plagues. So, while the recapitulation of Biblical history is not the chief purpose of *Revelation*, without an understanding of it a valid interpretation of *Revelation* is impossible.

The *"testimony"* of *Revelation* which the Church needs to hear is inextricably related to prophecies pertaining to the end time. A striking example of this would be the many prophetic passages in *Revelation* related to the fall of Babylon, which I understand to be the code word that John uses for all expressions of the pride of man that relate to the godless mechanisms and monuments of his philosophy and accomplishments, which are under the dominion of the forces of evil in the universe.

While we must engage in the noble task of interpreting these passages in the light of other Biblical references and in keeping with the historical purpose related to the Seven Churches of Asia, which is stated in 1:1a and repeated in the epilogue in 22:6, we must do so with the warning of Revelation 22:18-19 in mind: *"Now I bear solemn witness to every man who hears the words of the prophecy of this book: If anyone adds to these words, God will add to him the disasters described in this book; if anyone takes away from the words of prophecy in this book, God will take away from him his share in the tree of life and in the holy city which are described in this book."*

As I indicated in the introduction, one must not let this warning be a deterrence to an attempt to understand and interpret *Revelation*. Rather, it is a warning to anyone who disdains its testimony; uses its message to further his own agenda of power or personal gain; or who in pride would claim that his interpretation represents a flawless understanding of the mysteries that have been revealed.

What is the essence of the *"testimony for the Churches"* encoded in the historical-prophetic visions given by the angel of Jesus to John as he was in the Spirit, 1:10; 4:2; 17:3; 21:10? The triumphant testimony proclaimed in *Revelation* is: Jesus, the Lamb, is His Church's Bright Morning Star. As such He gives Himself in intimate fellowship to His Church, 2:28. The morning star speaks of the ability to illumine and is the harbinger of a new dawning. To

the ancient mind it also symbolized sovereignty. These characteristics of the morning star are illustrated by Piero della Francesca's
painting, *"The Resurrection."*

"The Resurrection," Piero della Francesca,
c. 1460, Pinacoteca Comunale, Borgo San Sepolcro

This painting, which the philosopher Aldous Huxley called *"the
greatest painting in the world,"* depicts the sovereignty of the risen
Christ. His left foot is on the tomb, which looks more like an
altar. Indeed, His wounds visible in the painting remind us of His
sacrifice. In Jesus' right hand is a staff holding high a cross banner
of victory. His piercing eyes and the centrality of His person add
to the sense of Jesus' sovereign power.

The sense that Jesus is the Morning Star, bringing a new dawn
and illumination, is in the painting as well. The sky would indicate that day is dawning. It would seem that the painting is also
meant to convey the idea of spiritual illumination, albeit in a subtle
way. The person whose head is in front of Jesus' garment and near

His left foot is the painter himself. In this way he seems to be indicating that he has been illuminated by the Morning Star. His face is of the same pinkish hue as Jesus' garment, and in contrast to the other figures, the turn of his head is seen in relationship to the person of Jesus.

Through John's eyes we have seen the *Revelation of Jesus Christ* as pointing to the One worthy of receiving *"glory, honor, and power"*. Let us take comfort in and heed the warnings of the epilogue Revelation 22:6-21. As we conclude our reading of *Revelation*, let us focus on the promises of Jesus stated or inferred in 22:6-7, 12-14, 20a. Let us hear the warnings stated or inferred in 22:8-11, 15, 18-19.

Above all, as faithful representatives of the Church let us proclaim Jesus who declared, *"I am both the root and stock of David, and the bright star of the morning!"* Revelation 22:16b. Let us join our witness with that of the Spirit and the Church universal by inviting the thirsty to drink of the *"water of life"*. *"The Spirit and the Bride say, 'Come!' Let everyone who hears this also say, 'Come!' Let the thirsty man come, and let everyone who wishes take the water of life as a gift,"* Revelation 22:17.

To the promise of Jesus, *"Yes, I am coming very quickly!"* let us respond, *"Amen, come, Lord Jesus!"* Revelation 22:20.

Also, during the interim period of waiting and witnessing before His coming, as children of the new covenant established by Jesus of the *"stock of David"* and *"the bright star of the morning,"* let us rejoice in the *"grace... given us in Christ Jesus before the beginning of time,"* II Timothy 1:9b, remembering that *"we are the temple of the living God; as God said, 'I will live in them and walk among them, and I will be their God, and they will be my people,'"* II Corinthians 6:16 NRSV.

The Almighty God and the Lamb are the New Jerusalem's Temple, 21:22, and Jesus has made believers the *"temple of the living God."* As such we can be faithful witnesses through the cleansing power of Jesus. The last beatitude of Revelation is: *"Happy are those who wash their robes, for they have the right to the tree of life and the freedom of the gates of the city,"* Revelation 22:14.

In the light of these promises related to purity, it is appropriate that we heed the admonition of II Corinthians 7:1: *"Since we have these promises, dear friends, let us purify ourselves from everything that contaminates body and spirit, perfecting holiness out of reverence for God."* The sanctifying grace of Jesus will enable us to purify ourselves. Like the Church at Sardis, each member of the Church today needs to be awake and sanctified. Then Jesus says, *"Indeed I will speak his name openly in the presence of my Father and of his angels,"* Revelation 3:5b. When Jesus speaks the names of His children openly before the Father, then the Church's Alpha will also be seen as its Omega. It is fitting that in 22:13 of the epilogue Jesus introduced Himself as *"Alpha and Omega, the First and the Last, the Beginning and the End."*

John's prayer in Revelation 22:21, that grace be given the struggling saints of his day, is his benediction for us as well: *"The grace of the Lord Jesus be with all his people."* By Jesus' grace His Beloved City will be with Him forevermore. Amen.

To order additional copies of

Fire From The Sky

please send
$9.95 plus
$3.00 shipping and handling to:

Lloyd Austin Phillips
2486 US 12 E
Niles, MI 49120
(616) 683-2786

(MI residents add 6% for state sales tax)